Nautical Twilight

The Story of a
Cape Cod Fishing Family

J. J. DUTRA

ISBN: 1463617747
ISBN-13: 9781463617745

Library of Congress Control Number: 2011910512
CreateSpace, North Charleston, South Carolina

NAUTICAL TWILIGHT

Nautical Twilight tells of one family's struggle to remain in the commercial fishing business from their summer days scalloping in Cape Cod Bay to their winter nights fishing the Atlantic Ocean. A Provincetown fishing memoir draws from the true life adventures of a Cape Cod fishing family. From total freedom to the systematic demise of the inshore fishing fleets, the story remembers fishing and fishermen at their zenith and is told through the eyes of a fisherman's wife. Nautical twilight is the period of time where it becomes less dark before sunrise — and darker after sunset — with the sun's center to twelve degrees under the horizon. The world of commercial fishing has changed, but the people who love the watermen's life have not.

ABOUT THE AUTHOR

The author lives in North Truro, Massachusetts with her husband and family. Together they have owned, worked and lived aboard a variety of fishing and sailing vessels. They currently own the F/V *Richard & Arnold*.

www.provincetownfishwife.com

CONTENTS

ACKNOWLEDGEMENTS

It is with great appreciation that I acknowledge those who have given me what I most needed. Thank you to all the many crewmen who have worked with us. To: Mary Hutchings, Angela Caruso, Madonna Tasha, Sarah Hutchings, Joe and Chrissy Amaral, Christine Wold, Susan Jahnig, Steve Kennedy - thank you for your help and support. My apprication to Joyce Tracksler for your encouragement, Professor Brooks Landon for inspiring longer sentences, Joe Stollenwork for moving me forward and special thanks to the many Dutras: Jackson, Robert, Nicole, Bernadette for believing in me and thanks to David, Olivia, Alex, and Ryan for providing me with laughter and unconditional love. And to my biggest fan - Dave - without whom there would be no Nautical Twilight — thanks for the memories.

This book is dedicated to all the fishermen who have crossed the decks of the following Provincetown fishing boats:

The Captain Bill, The Patricia Marie, Victory, Three of Us, Francis Elizabeth, Reneva, Jennifer & Aaron, Jenny M, Fanny Parnel, Victory II, Shirley & Roland, the New England, John David, Nancy B, Victoria, Deborah H, Nancy & Rickey, Three n' One, Kathy Jo, Loretta R, Lillian C, Stella, Sol-A-Mar, Revenge, Rosemary, Yankee, Santa Theresa, El Mario, Daisy T, Papa Joe, the Cape Cod, Pilheria, Martha Lee, Peter & Linda, Josephine G, Jimmy Boy, Little Natalia, the North Star, Petrel, Strider, Bay of Isles, Little Chuck, Bonanza, Triumph, Mary Madelyn, Perry Bros, Cormorant, Harbor Bar, Nordic, Eleanor, Laura, Sonya, Sea Fox, Bacalhau, James M. Burke, Brother Joe, Judy & Tony, Mary & Madeline, Porpoise, Johnny O, Miss Sandy, Ruthie L. Michael & Amy, Liberty Bell, Eastern Star, Magellan, Kathy Jo, Charlotte G, Jerusalem, Galaxy, B-Tri-O, Patricia Ann, Plymouth Bell, Sarah Lynn, Gail, Gale Winds, Silver Mink, Lebenth, Raiders, Santina, Barracuda, Polo Marc, Alwa, Down-easter, Little Infant, Wanderer, Zerta, Ocean Spray, Wellington, Revenge, Atlanta, Dolora M, Queen Mary, Caroline, Sea Runt, Francis & Marion, Aerolite, Lillian B, Mary M, Razor's Edge, Joan & Tom, Emelia R, Clara M, Dawn, Wallace & Ray, Melene II, Jenny B, Alice J, Shelia, P-town Queen, Cape Star, Sea Star, Sea Fox, Barbara Lee, Barbara Ann, Menco, Katherine Marie, Cutty's Ark, Southern Cross, Esther M, Viola D, Jessie Dutra, Pat Sea, Sea Butcher, Big Red, the Wildflower, the Kingfisher

INTRODUCTION

Dave should have been jumping for joy, whooping and thanking the fish gods when he saw the codfish sticking out of the net as it popped to the surface behind his old dragger, instead he wanted to scream in anger and frustration. He grabbed his cell phone from the dashboard in the pilot-house and called the National Marine Fisheries Service in Gloucester, Massachusetts reaching an anonymous woman and telling her that he had six thousand pounds of codfish on his deck, begging her to let him keep the fish. "Please, there must be something you can do," Dave said.

Her answer was calm as if she'd crossed the path of irate fishermen before. "You are allowed eight hundred pounds for the day or you can stay out for seven days then unload the catch." Dave explained that he was all alone; he had two sandwiches and a pint of milk on board, there was no way he could stay off shore for a week on his eighty year old boat. "I'm sorry. The regulations say you can only have eight hundred pounds for the day," she explained. "It's a changing world, sir.

There was bitterness in Dave's reply, "You want me to throw these fish back dead? It may be a changing world, but there is right and there is wrong - and this is wrong." He hung his head as he pushed the off button on the phone. Rather than scream and rant, he contacted me at home. "Call everyone we know who has a boat in the water. Tell them I'll be on the three mile line off the New Beach for the next few hours." Dave continued, "Tell them if they want eight hundred pounds of cod fish to come and get them." I heard him curse before he hung up. Six boats showed up and the captain gave away all his catch. Dave wondered if he might be committing a crime by giving away the fish, but there was no doubt in his mind that the National Marine Fisheries Service was committing a sin by making regulations that forced fishermen to throw dead fish overboard.

In its rush to reach sustainability the NMFS has used criteria that make it impossible for small businesses to survive. Fishing history is being used to determine our fishing future. What does history mean to you? Our boat's fishing history dates to 1927 and our permit history began then. The NE Regional Administrator, Ms. Pat Kurkul, stated in 'Commercial Fisheries News' January 2011 "Landings data are a vessel's legacy and establish its fishing history." But instead of using our vessel's many years of catching fish, NMFS is using fish-catch data collected from the years 1996 to 2006 in deciding on the allocation. What that means is that no other history is taken into account. For many fishermen it means the end of fishing. Is it possible to erase our boat's history, leaving us without a future?

David and I have been involved in the fisheries for decades. We have always obeyed the rules, never wanting more than our share. We have watched catch limits, control dates, and many hundreds of regulations remove countless small fishing businesses from our waters. Provincetown, Massachusetts has a rich fishing history that dates back centuries and yet most of its fishing fleet has disappeared during the past twenty years. The Provincetown fleet is now a shadow of what once was a thriving fishing community. To understand the current state of our fishery a person would have had to work, as we have, from the deck of a commercial fishing boat for thirty-five years. We've seen the best of fishing, the worst of it, the humor and the heartache. We embrace change for without it there is no life, but the changes now occurring in the world of commercial fishing are staggering, unnatural and un-American. We are aware of the politics, the sciences, the environmental impacts and the social implications of giving the fishery to a few — putting all the fish in the hands of corporate control.

It hasn't always been this way. We began our fishing days knowing total freedom, when we thought we knew what was best for ourselves. How our simple way of life got to be so complicated is only part of the story. From our sunrise in the fishing industry to the sunset on the Provincetown fishing fleet Dave and I have been a part of the world of boats, fish and fishermen. There are a million parts to the conundrum of fishing, like a diamond, many faceted, or like the oceans, unfathomable.

CHAPTER 1

The 'Fanny Parnel'

Memories swirl in the mirrors of my mind like dune dust that whips across the tops of sand hills on a windy day as I visualize the green, gray and blue of Cape Cod Bay and the fine tans of the sand upon which our lives have been built. I can see in my mirror the receding skyline of Provincetown as we head out of the harbor. Past Long Point Lighthouse and bell buoy number 3 the boat navigates into the expanse of Cape Cod Bay. Perhaps it is fall and we are going fishing for flounder or maybe it is winter and we have a rake on the boat and go in search of sea scallops. Squid calls us in spring and in summer our course is south, toward the fluke and lobster; for all can be seen in my mirror.

The images I recall are of a fleet of small boats heading away from the wharf, away from the lines that bind men to the land. It is just before dawn, nautical twilight and the fishing boats motor out of the harbor in a neat row. One after the other, lights on in the rigging, they are moving slowly toward the fishing ground to the West, North, East and South, around the peninsula shaped like an arm held up to show its might and muscle.

As the Provincetown fishing boats came and went from the harbor, I was working as a waitress at a local hang-out, the Surf Club. A chance encounter with a local fisherman took me in a direction that was totally unexpected. One evening in June a young man sat on a bar stool sipping a beer and when I mentioned that I was looking for a place to live, he said, "This is a tourist town; the dance of moving two times a year is one of the drawbacks of living here. If you rent and don't have a year round apartment, you move in June and October. My name is Dave, by the way." Our short conversation included the fact that he was fishing on a Provincetown dragger. "I have to be onboard the boat at four in the morning, so I'd better get going. I'll see you around." He left the restaurant and I thought about the guy for a minute before going back to serving hamburgers and beer.

A few days later a pick-up truck stopped beside me as I walked along Commercial Street. It was Dave. "Hey Jude, need a lift?" I remembered the conversation we'd had.

"I'm on my way to look at a year round rental, like you suggested the other night,"

His reply was a surprise, "My uncle Tootsie has a place for rent. Hop in. I'll take you there." His dark hair flopped on his forehead as he leaned across the front seat to open the truck door for me. "It's a small apartment, but take a look," he said. I didn't hesitate. The radio was playing a Beetles tune, 'Norwegian Wood', isn't it good, one of my favorites. A short ride led to an empty apartment - the place was the size of a matchbox. I didn't take his uncle Tootsie's apartment, renting instead the one I'd been heading for.

"How about coming with me to Hatches Harbor next Friday?" he asked during the ride. The white tee shirt sparkled against his tanned Portuguese skin.

Not knowing what Hatches Harbor was, yet knowing there was something about the way he smiled that made Hatches Harbor inviting I said, "Sure." We made arrangements to meet the following Friday and I was ready with towels and sandwiches when he showed up in his four-wheel drive Chevy truck. After he let the air out of the tires he turned the truck onto a sandy track. We crossed wind swept terrain while he told me about the light house keepers who had used this same sand road to bring supplies from town by horse and cart. "They climbed the lighthouse steps without fail every night to light the lamp, living weeks and sometimes months without seeing another soul." The beach grass, the brush, the scrub pine trees growing in groups among white sand appeared stunted and contorted by the ever present wind.

Dave seemed to know about the place, "In 1890 a lighthouse keeper logged twelve hundred ships passing Race Point in one twenty-four hour period. That's more boats than we see in a month." There were no other people, no cars, and no houses, only small hills of fine sand and blue sky. A sweet smell of roses floated in waves through the open windows. They seemed to grow in spite of their environment. Through the sunny windshield I caught views of the sea as it peeked from behind the dunes. The truck bounded from one rut to the next - sometimes jolting and sometimes causing us to lift off the seat with just enough momentum to give me the feeling of weightlessness. Dave knew just how fast to travel in order to keep us from tapping our heads on the ceiling of the truck cab.

"My friends and I drove our trucks all over the dunes while we were in high school," Dave said. "We had races out here."

"WOW, WHOA" I exclaimed. Other sounds of surprise and delight came from somewhere within me, girlish giggles emerged without notice.

Hatches Harbor turned out to be a small inlet not accessible to the usual traveler. Surrounded by dunes that gently slope, ending in a pool of ice cold Atlantic water, I wondered at its emptiness. The shifting sands form a barrier beach that changes with the coming and going of the ten foot tide. "The only way to reach this spot is via this remote sand road or by sea on a high tide," Dave gave me a verbal tour pointing toward the water. "In the hollows of the dunes blueberries, cranberries, raspberries, beach plums and wild peas grow," he said.

I wanted to stay and live in the lighthouse.

We parked close to the horseshoe shaped bowl of water. Our voices competing with the sound of the sea as it scratched and fizzled across the sand in front of us. "I'm building a boat in my dad's garage," he said. "Come by next week and I'll show it to you. You can ride your bike out; it's only a couple of miles from Provincetown." I listened to his directions, thinking I'd have to borrow a bike.

A few days later I was standing in the garage where a twenty- three foot Cape Ann Dory was taking shape. The building was tucked between a house and The Anchorage Motel on Beach Point in North Truro, on a busy stretch of road lined with motels and cottages that crowd the waterfront. The wooden boat frame took up the entire room with just enough space left to walk around it. Dave greeted me with a smile and pointed at the boat, "Lap-streaked," he said. "Flat-bottomed, the type used by the dory-men who fished with line and hooks on the Grand Banks in the 1800's, sturdy and sea-worthy."

I could see that a boat was taking shape. The double doors of the garage were open to let in the light. It looked like a jigsaw puzzle to me. The frame of a boat was suspended upside down on sawhorses. There were wood curlicues all over the floor. "I'm just attaching the ribs to the floor timbers." Dave explained as he gently touched various parts of the boat.

"It sure smells good in here," was all I could think to say. I had never seen anything like it.

"It's the cedar. I'm using it for the planks. The ribs are oak." He ran his hand over the wood and remarked, "Every piece of wood used to make the boat has a name. This is the keel, here at the bottom, the garboards are next, then ribs and then planks are fixed to form the vessel. Lap-streaked means the wood will run from stem to stern overlapping the plank below it all the way up the sides. It's double-ended; kind of pointed on both ends."

He unfolded some papers, "I'm following a set of plans, called offsets. Let me show you." The half hour lesson in boat building proved enlightening but I was paying more attention to the muscles of his arms, the way he moved and the concentration that registered on his bearded face. The sheets of drawings were a pattern for the frame on the stands, but not as interesting as his frame. He told me about his soon to-be boat and his dreams of sailing her in Cape Cod Bay. I didn't understand much, but I sure loved his enthusiasm. My senses heightened, the atmosphere seemed heavy with more than the cedar. He moved slightly away from me and asked, "How about I meet you later tonight?"

I held my breath then said, "Yes, that would be nice." Just then Dave's mom appeared in the doorway with a pile of sheets in her arms. She narrowed her eyes, squinting into the boat shop. When she asked Dave to give her a hand he said he'd be right there and we said good-bye. I headed back to town with my stomach filled with butterflies.

Just before closing time there he was sitting on the same bar stool. After leaving the restaurant we pushed our bikes through the busy tourist town. "Have you named the dory you're building?" I asked.

He smiled, "I'm going to call it '*Fanny Parnel*' after the boat my father and grandfather fished back in the 1930's and 40's. I don't remember the boat, because I was little when it left town." He went on to explain that many boats are named for women. "As far as I know there was no real Fanny Parnel, but my grandfather spent so much time fishing and was never home that my grandmother called her 'the other woman'. I guess Fanny was her competition."

We eased our way through the crowds of people which thinned as we distanced ourselves from the town center. I was full of questions; asking what he did when not working on the dory, about growing up in Provincetown and about his family.

"I'm working aboard the 'Jenny M' right now. She's a dragger that has been fishing out of Provincetown since before World War II. Ray Duarte owns the boat and I work as crew." He slowed his bike. "Do you eat fish?" he asked. When I told him I did, he said he'd bring me some from the next trip out.

Dave had spent his life around the wharfs and alleyways of this town that I was beginning to love. I wanted to know more. Dave looked at the ground as we walked, "I wish I'd known my father and grandfather, but they both died when I was just a baby. I was kind of adopted by the town's fishermen after my father died. I was on boats by the time I was ten years old. It was part of growing up here." We arrived at my door.

I asked him in and the compelling and mysterious dance of summer love began. He was fishing and I was working two jobs, but we made time to ride bikes, go swimming and spend time getting to know one another. In August he told me he was launching the dory. "Come by Saturday morning and watch the activities," he said. "We'll try and get it into the water on the high tide about ten o'clock." I rode my borrowed bike to North Truro and walked out to the beach in front of the motel at the appointed time.

An amazing sight greeted me. The freshly painted white dory sat on the sand with Cape Cod Bay one hundred feet away. A small crowd had gathered to see how this hand made, twenty-three foot boat would move to the water. David introduced me to his mom and dad who owned the motel and then to his friends, Bobby Weiser and Richard Goldberg who were on hand to help. I watched as Dave placed planks on the sand in front of the boat at the width of the dory, and then round pipes were laid horizontally across the planks. The dory rolled forward as Dave, Bobby and Richard hustled, moving the pipes from the back of the boat to the front. The 'Fanny Parnel' was making her first journey.

The white double-ended boat traveled slowly across the sand ending in the rising surf. A mooring line with a buoy was attached to a cleat on the bow. "Now what," I asked.

"Now we wait," Dave said. The others left and Dave and I sat on the beach waiting for the tide to lift the boat. Slowly water made its way toward our feet. I was alarmed to see that the dory was filling with water, leaking from every seam, eventually wallowing. I thought I would cry.

Dave saw the expression of horror on my face and put his arm around my shoulder, "Don't worry. The planks have got to swell. The wood is dry and the seams are open. Wait and see. She'll not leak a drop in a couple of days."

I left the beach thinking, "What a bummer." Disappointed, I wasn't even sure I wanted to see the boat again, but I did return and there it was - bobbing on the mooring. David was putting an anchor and line aboard. A mast and stay wires had been added since my last visit. "Are you ready for a sail," he asked?

"I'm as ready as I'll ever be," I said as I waded into the water. Dave held my hand gently pulling me over the rail and into the floating craft. When I was settled on a bench amidships, Dave let go the mooring warp, freeing us from the land. He raised a sail and we began to move as I rid myself of any lingering doubts.

We talked as the boat tacked toward the Pilgrim Monument seven miles away. Time seemed to cease as we glided toward the far shore. Halfway across the bay I thought of Winslow Homer. I was living the painting. The dory moved with grace, through and on and in-between the water. I had never sailed a boat before and was thrilled when Dave put the tiller in my hands. For me her maiden voyage was a success, so when Dave said, "I'm thinking of selling her" I was shocked and surprised, but then he went on to say, "She's not big enough." This dory was not the work of my hands, so I didn't have a vote in what would happen to it.

I surveyed the vessel in which I sat and loved the look and feel of it. "You did a fine job building this boat."

"Thanks," was all he said.

Coming to Provincetown by boat is enchanting. The Pilgrim Monument, the town and the wharfs are reflected in the water. The main pier was crowded with fishing boats and I could see names painted on the bows and sterns as we drifted past. At first glance the boats all looked alike, dark green with nets hanging from the masts, but then I noticed each was unique. Different colors, different decorations and shapes gave each vessel a distinction. "Look, that boat has a Christmas tree at the top of the mast," I pointed to the nearest fishing boat.

"That's Louie Rivers' boat the *'Johnny O.'* He changes that tree after Christmas each year." Dave pointed to other draggers, "See the *'Patricia Marie'*, the black boat over there, Billy King painted Playboy bunny ears on the bow." I looked at the hulls and David continued, "The *'Jerusalem'* has the Star of David, and see the *'Liberty'* she has the head of the Statue of Liberty painted on the bow. The *'Barracuda'* has sharks teeth. Not all the boats have that sort of decoration, but they're all unique." We coasted past the wharf with its fleet of boats and headed toward the beach. "I'd like to own my own dragger someday. I'm looking around for a boat that I can fish by myself, but I haven't found it yet." His cheerful eyes looked at me as he shared this dream. I saw confidence there and something else, hope perhaps.

Dave dropped the sail as the flat bottomed boat came to a stop on the beach. "I don't know that I would be able to part with this little beauty, but I have a feeling you'll find the right boat. Right now let's celebrate the maiden voyage of the *'Fanny Parnel'*. Come on, I'll buy you a beer," I thanked him for a lovely day.

A couple of weeks later he took me fishing with him aboard the *'Jenny M'*. My first fishing trip got me out of bed at 3 a.m. with enthusiasm. With Dave's guidance I found myself on the deck of the forty-eight foot dragger. It was smaller than I had expected and the motion was disorienting, but I soon learned why people love the sea. An hour into the trip I watched a whale breech twenty feet from the side of the boat, the water appeared every shade of blue, and the air smelled sweeter than I could have imagined.

Dave fixed a seat for me by turning a wooden fish box upside down. From there I watched the sea, the boat and the sky. I was told to stay out of the way and when I asked if I could help, the captain said, "Women don't work on Portuguese boats. Matter of fact some captains think having women on board is bad luck." Ray's smile said otherwise. "But not me, I like having women around."

After an hour, the captain brought the boat into a tight circle, bringing the net close to the side of the boat at midship, between two iron frames that they called 'gallows'. Ray hollered, "Haul Back." When the net was close enough, a rope with a hook on the end was placed into the 'splitting strap' and the captain turned on the wench. The line looped around a piece of gear called the 'capstan' that pulled it up through a block and tackle. The boat tilted a few degrees as it rolled in the swell, pulled down toward the heavy net. Raising from the water the net reminded me of an onion bag, only much bigger, hanging in the air. It cleared the rail, and then with a loud squishing sound the net landed on the deck. I could see a knot of some kind on the very bottom that Dave yanked with a sharp tug. Hundreds of pounds of fish, sand, debris, shells, sticks and all sorts of things I'd never imagined existed fell to the deck. The men went to work picking through the salty deposit.

After the net was emptied, it was pushed back over the side as the boat pulled away, letting it disappear into the blue-green-gray water. Wooden boxes were placed near the pile. I saw wiggling creatures emerging from the sand and mud. The men dug through the jumble of living matter, throwing fish into boxes: one box for sea scallops, one for lobsters, one for crabs, one for yellow-tail flounder and one for everything else.

I moved closer to Dave and he told me to watch out for goosefish and dog fish, "They have sharp teeth and can give a nasty bite. You have to wear gloves and boots to protect your-self if you dig through the pile. Some of these critters can give you nasty wounds." He told me a story about a man he worked with that got something in his eye from the pile that was dumped on deck. "The crewman wound up at Massachu-setts General Hospital with an eye infection; the worse they had ever seen. He almost lost his sight." I looked at my san-dals and stepped back from the mass of sea bottom as the boat rolled and I lost my balance. Dave held me steady and I felt rescued, safe, yet somehow timid in this new environment.

The routine went on all day while I breathed in the salt air and watched sea gulls swoop. Stretching out on the forward deck of the gently rocking boat I felt more alive than I had ever thought possible as I stared into the mysterious sea. At noon Dave brought me lunch on a paper plate from out of the foc'sle. It was fried fish and potatoes. I couldn't tell whether it was the salt air, the excitement or the freshness, but I'd never tasted anything so good. While I sat eating the fine lunch, Dave told me he sold the 'Fanny Parnel'. "I don't have time for sailing right now. I built it mostly to see if I could do it. I know now it isn't big enough and besides, this is what I really want, fishing my own boat." I looked at him and understood exactly what he meant.

"Somehow I know you'll find it," I said.

Dave looked around the boat and asked, "What do you think of it?"

I said, "This is the most amazing thing I've ever done." Little did I know that day onboard the *'Jenny M'* that the romance of the sea would fill my future. I was in love with the ocean, fishing and David.

CHAPTER 2

The 'Wildflower'

My decision to stay the winter was the beginning of a lifelong love. I couldn't leave this peninsula, the boats and the town. It was a magical place. Dave and I continued to date on and off for a year. I was not in a hurry to make any changes; things seemed to be going fine. One day while I was at the stove making chocolate pudding he came up behind me, put his arms around my waist and asked if I would marry him. With chocolate dripping onto my hand I said, "When?"

"Anytime you want," Dave said.

I didn't take a moment to answer, "How about next week?" It was a snap decision, but I never doubted that I was doing the right thing – following my heart.

Dave continued fishing with Raymond on the '*Jenny M*', I got a job at the school and we moved into a bigger apartment near the center of town. We'd been married for a year and I was pregnant with our first child when Dave came home, announcing that he had found a boat and wanted me to see it. I made us a cup of tea while with a rush of excitement he began telling me everything, "It was probably built for fishing, but someone tried to make it a live-aboard. She has a shallow draft, forty-two feet long and has great potential and we can get it cheap." I didn't say anything and he continued, "With a little work I think I could be fishing by next winter. This is our chance to have our own fishing boat."

There was no way I'd curb his enthusiasm besides it was infectious, so I agreed to see what he was talking about. After a one hour trip to Hyannis, I sat in the truck looking at an abandoned boat that reminded me of a giant sea gull: body comfortably deep amidships with its tail turned up into the air and a wheelhouse where the head would be. I'd seen pictures in magazines of fishing boats similar to this one that worked the northern waters of Nova Scotia from the Bay of Fundy to the coast of Maine; they were known as Novi boats.

This vessel sat at the back of a 'bone yard', like an elephant graveyard for boats. It appeared in dire need of repair. "It's going to take a bit of work." Dave stepped from the truck to show me this hulk of wood. "I knew when I spotted her that she had good lines and was worth the effort needed to bring her back to useable condition and besides it really is cheap." At twenty seven years of age all things are possible. He had the energy, the drive, and some knowledge of the fishing business; I figured I'd see what developed. I would be able to keep working until the baby was born; Dave could continue to fish with Raymond and spend his off time making his possible dream come true, besides where else would we find a fishing boat for $500.

We talked over supper about how he pictured this boat fitted out, "I want to get her up and fishing as fast as possible, there's so much to be done," he said. I thought about how happy I was being his wife and how fishing his own boat might provide us with the income to have a home of our own someday. I knew there was money to be made. David was now getting a share of the catch, about twenty percent of the total from Ray. It only made sense to have the other eighty percent come to our home. I looked at the boat as an investment in our future.

Dave began driving to Hyannis every chance he got to get the boat ready for the water. Made of long planks that meet at the butt ends and are fastened to a frame of oak ribs, the hull appeared in decent condition. David used 'Boat-Life' and a caulking gun to fill each seam that had shrunk from drying and were opening. The boat took on the appearance of a zebra as white stripes of gook squeezed out of a tube ran along every plank from stem to stern. After a week of intense activity around the boat we sat in Dave's truck following a big travel-lift, tractor truck carrying our forty-two foot boat down the road to be launched at Sesuit Harbor in Dennis. From where I sat the hull looked like a washed out, paint peeling mass of old wood with stripes. I was apprehensive but kept quiet.

"What am I thinking?" Dave was wide-eyed. I stared at him, silent and confused as he continued, "It's too late now. I'll just get her in the water and take it home. It's a short trip across the bay, just twenty miles." He relaxed a bit, taking deep breaths. "Peter will be here in a couple of days with his boat the '*Sea Butcher*' and tow us home."

The driver maneuvered the boat around and before Dave could change his mind, she was going backward down a ramp. The trailer tipped its bottom down, the boat slid gently off into the water and the truck was gone, leaving us alone in the parking lot at sunset on a cold December afternoon. Dave had a rope fastened to the bow which he then attached to a wharf pole, securing the boat which seemed to shrink when it entered the water. There was not another boat, car or person to be seen. Dave told me to stay in the truck while he connected a battery to the pump in the bilge, the lowest point of the boat's hull, where the water settles. He heard a trickle of water coming into the bottom, but just a small sound that seemed manageable with the pump. Dave added more lines to the wharf, looked her over again, and then we headed for home. "I hate leaving her there, but we're both tired. We can come back early in the morning," he said.

We returned to the harbor in the predawn hours of nautical twilight. With the lights of his truck aimed toward the spot where his boat was tied, Dave leaned over the wood piling, seeing the roof of the wheelhouse about four feet below him and nothing else. The shape of the boat was a shadow against the dark water and sky. Dave jumped to the roof of the wheelhouse and then to the deck. I heard a cracking, splintering sound and was horrified to hear yelling, "I can't get my foot free. The boat's full of water. Find a rope in the truck and tie it to wharf pole, then drop it down to me. I'll use it to pull myself up." His voice echoed in the still air. His weight had caused the boat to lean over because her belly was full of water. She was swamped.

I was terrified to leave him, but I did as he asked. It took effort to pull his leg out and I worried that the boat would roll over before he could get free. I watch as he pulled himself from the deck to the top of the wheelhouse and then to the wharf.

"You're bleeding," I said.

"Never mind that, I'm not hurt. We'll fix my leg later." He was looking back at his new purchase. The boat was completely awash. With hands clenched at his sides he said, "The tide's going out; we have a few hours before the water will be up again. Let's get busy." Daylight was seeping into the small harbor as all the water seeped out of the boat. There it sat on the sandy bottom tied to the wharf like a pet waiting for directions.

"She looks like a big wooden bath tub, with the plug out." I laughed with relief.

"I'll be under the boat to see what kind of problems we have and I'll put a hole in her belly. I've got to let the water out before I can fix the leaks." He managed to sound optimistic. Water was running out from a big seam near the garboard plank, where the keel meets the bottom; the garboard is sometimes called the 'devil' and for good reason. "I'll have just enough time to give her a quick patch-up with more boat-life, add another pump and another battery and hopefully get her to float." He added, "Well, I knew she wasn't perfect when

I got her." He sent me into town to pick up coffee, donuts and some big Band-Aids.

I patched his leg and then he patched up the boat. When the tide came up, the boat floated as if nothing had happened that morning. "Looks like it'll be safe here for a while." Dave said. "You must be tired. I'll take you home. I'll come back after supper and stay aboard, just in case."

After a fretful night I could hear the relief in his voice when he called to tell me everything was ok. "I've hooked up another battery and a second pump, but she's not leaking very much. I'll be home for supper." It was my turn to feel relief.

Dave spent the next two days making phone calls and checking the tide chart while he kept an eye on his new purchase. Peter Morris showed up in his 40 ft lobster boat ready for action. There was not a breath of wind when Peter hollered out across the still water, "Looks like a good day for a tow." Peter was a true Cape Codder, born and raised in Truro he had years of experience on the water, serving in the Merchant Marine during the Korean conflict, spending time on ships all over the world. His six foot frame and strong muscles had served him well for working on scallop boats, long-liners that used lines with hooks and now his own fishing boat that he fished with his wife Pat. She and I sat in the truck as a back-up support team for our men. They would tow the boat and we would bring the truck home.

The 'Sea Butcher's engine had had a recent overhaul, but the exhaust was spewing black diesel soot across the sky. Pete said, "Don't worry about that smoke. It'll clear." Dave had enough on his mind with tow ropes and keeping the derelict afloat to worry about other problems. Anxious excitement kept Dave moving about like a flea. They tied the two boats side by side while inside the small harbor. Once they were in the open waters of Cape Cod Bay the tow line was moved to the stern. A rope stretched twenty feet between the two boats as they headed northeast toward Truro.

Dave took a deep breath, looked at his new boat behind them and then up into the sky above, either checking the weather or saying a prayer. He could see a line of brown smoke hanging in the air - going straight across the bay. Peter had a smile on his face when he said, "We can just follow my trail all the way back to Pamet Harbor."

One hour into the tow, in the middle of the bay, the muffler on the 'Sea Butcher' caught fire - just burst into flames. Adding to the excitement of the already exhausting launching, Dave wasn't sure if he would need to abandon ship and swim to the one at the end of the tow line. Peter calmly picked up the deck hose and sprayed salt water onto the fiery mass, dousing the flames. He joked, "Happens when she gets hot, sort-of like my redheaded wife." He gave a laugh and popped open a 'Pabst-Blue-Ribbon'.

A swift tide helped pull the boats into an empty Pamet Harbor, only a few balls bobbing to mark anchors. Dave grabbed a mooring in the deepest part of the small bowl. Peter's wife Pat and I sat waiting and watching from the truck. We could see the line of smoke that followed our men back home. When the new / old boat was secured to a mooring

Peter put the *'Sea Butcher'* on another and then used his skiff to pick up Pat and me, rowing us back to the latest addition to the fleet. Dave was busy checking the bilge, looking her over. Peter tied the skiff. We climbed aboard and sat on the rail of our new floating vessel. Dave sat down next to us and let out an audible sigh. "Welcome to the world of boat ownership," Peter said and gave Dave a thump on the back. We enjoyed a beer then Dave took Peter and Pat back to land, keeping the skiff for our use.

We stayed onboard that night with an oil lamp, a bottle of wine, a couple of sandwiches and sleeping bags. I wanted to be a part of this adventure. Dave lit a fire in the pot belly stove left from her live-aboard days, using some old newspaper and the legs of a chair. We snuggled and talked about his plans for this boat. To keep from freezing we burned all the furnishings - tables, chairs and anything that wasn't needed to keep her afloat. Above our heads the December wind howled, while our little cabin got downright cozy. Dave was up every hour checking the bilge. The pumps were keeping up with any leakage and I felt safe, a trusting of the unknown. The boat swayed to and fro as the wind pushed and pulled. The slapping of the rippling water against the hull was new to me and vexing. I slept fitfully. When I mentioned it to Dave he said he didn't hear it. "You'll get used to it," he said and I knew then that I'd be spending more time onboard.

In the morning Pete came by to inspect Dave's new boat and lend a helping hand. He gave Dave one of his big smiles, a thumbs-up and said, "Not bad. She's going need just a little work here and there, but I can see you'll be fishing alongside the '*Sea Butcher*' next summer." They rechecked the pump, looked into the bilges, and proclaimed her fit. Dave and Peter congratulated each other, the leaks were under control. We headed for home. She'd not sink today. Arrangements were made to have her hauled out of the water in two days' time.

It was during the second night in Pamet Harbor that the old wreck of a boat made her way silently, up and over the banking like a cat at night stalking unsuspecting prey. While we slept at home in pure abandonment, the wind picked up to gale force and blew from the Northeast throughout the night. That boat left her mooring, slipping over the marsh grass, skittering across the land for a hundred feet and coming to rest, high and dry, overlooking a meadow of clam flats and mud gullies. She was a vision of loveliness and would have been the making of many a Cape Cod painting if she had remained there.

Pamet Harbor is a very small basin flanked by marshland, estuary and the Pamet River with a small opening to Cape Cod Bay. Its beauty is unforgettable, bringing people from around the world. Into this little gully of a harbor, moorings are squeezed. During the summer months, the sterns and bows of small vessels at anchor swing with precision and you can easily pass the time of day with your neighbor. But the harbor is deserted during the winter, only hearty souls play with boats in December.

Dave and I arrived at the Pamet Harbor at daylight. There she was - not on the mooring where we had left her, but up on the marsh! Dave stared for a few minutes, scratching his head, muttering to himself. "Maybe I should forget everything and drive away? Damn," he said. I said nothing, feeling crushing defeat.

He turned the truck around and drove to Peter and Pat's home. The four of us crowed into the truck cab staring out at the boat that the men had worked to save only twenty-four hours before. "What are you going to do?" Pete asked. "Let her go by way of many shipwrecked vessels?"

"Not likely. It's been too much work this far to let it go now. Besides I paid good money for it." Dave said

They talked it over, "Do you think we can pull her off"

"Yup"

"Got any line long enough?"

"Nope, but let's see what kind of help we can get" Dave said. The beginning of a plan was hatching and the men knew they were in this together.

"I'm not sure the 'Sea Butcher' has enough power to get her back in the water and I don't have a rope long enough." Peter was slowly shaking his head.

I could see a steely determination come over Dave, a side of him I'd not seen before. "I'm going to town to talk with the local Coast Guard. See if they can help." Dave said. They made plans to meet later in the day and to keep in touch via phone. As it turned out the local Coast Guardsmen were in need of some practice, so a drill, a rescue would be a good thing. I wondered if Dave explained to the Chief the full details, that this vessel was just a plank away from being a derelict, but it didn't matter, their adrenaline was up and it was time to save the ship.

I had just read Farley Mowat's book *Gray Seas Under* and it explains rescuing vessels of much larger proportions, tankers and container ships, so I thought that in comparison our rescue would be a piece of cake. The United States Coast Guard showed up in Pamet Harbor aboard their thirty foot cutter at about three in the afternoon. All hands were dressed in orange wilderness survival suits. Peter and Dave arrived by truck in time to see the small cutter come in through the jetties. Pat and I were there in the other truck to 'stand-by', as Dave put it. He had made it clear that we were to stay out of the way.

A full moon tide had filled the small basin, overflowing the banks, giving the illusion that the harbor was larger than it really was. There was water everywhere. The Coast Guard vessel appeared to be floating inside a huge open harbor. The sun would be setting in less than an hour and the harbor looked magical as a full moon appeared over our shoulders. With professional ease and knowledgeable experience, the guardsmen proceeded to back the cutter up toward the stricken hulk that lay slightly askew up on the marsh, one hundred yards away. The temperature hovered around twenty degrees and the air was crystal clear. There was a light wind from the Northwest.

Dave and Peter got out of the truck and walked down the ramp to the skiff, their breaths coming out, in soft white clouds while their eyes scanned the harbor. They watched the white cutter with the orange strip turn its bow up into the wind with the stern moving toward the stricken vessel. "They made it here a lot quicker than I thought they would," Pete said.

Tops of marsh grass poked through the frozen landscape as Pat and I enjoyed the pristine natural environment, excited about the rescue. While out in the harbor, in order to move closer to the wayward boat, the powerful engines of the rescue cutter began to throttle up - in reverse. I could hear the revving sound across the harbor echoing against the surrounding dunes. Dave and Peter realized at the same time what was about to happen. They started waving their arms and hollering to let the rescuers know that they had put themselves in peril. Their boat was clawing its way, using the propeller and powerful engines to climb up and over the submerged mud bank.

The group of rescuers suddenly found themselves caught up in eelgrass and churning mud. The Guardsman at the helm must have thought there was a lot of water under them, so he throttled up even more. Things happen quickly on the water. The marsh was now under them.

Peter and Dave, trying to get the Coast Guard's attention were hollering and waving their arms, but the roar of the V671 was thunderous as the captain put the engines in full ahead then full reverse trying to get back into deep water. The two on shore wasted no time and launched a small skiff. Dave threw in the oars and began rowing. Just then the revving engines stalled and the harbor became ominously quiet.

The tide was beginning to turn. Dave pulled on the oars, but they didn't seem to be getting anywhere. On the other side of the basin, the white boat was just beginning to lean to starboard as the Pamet Harbor began its race out into Cape Cod Bay. I've heard that cold slows thinking, so because of the excitement and adrenaline pumping, it took a few seconds for Dave to discover that he wasn't making any headway, no forward motion because the shaft of the outboard engine was caught on a mooring warp. He had to back-water while Peter freed them from the snarl.

As the saying goes, 'Time and tide wait for no man'. Dave and Pete made it to the side of the Coast Guard vessel in time to hear someone hollering. "OH SHIT, OH SHIT, OH SHIT!" Without the motor roaring his voice was clearly audible throughout the harbor. A young man was moving rapidly from wheelhouse to stern with a long sounding pole. He was using the gaff to probe the water on both sides of the boat. "Oh shit, oh shit, oh shit" came the call across the water.

The rescue boat was half on the marsh and half in the water. The port side had a foot of water under it and the starboard side had 6 feet, the tide was out going and the tide can leave the most remarkable objects in its wake. The icy water was getting closer to the rail as the boat tipped toward it. Dave yelled to a young man near to the bow, "Give me the longest line you have onboard. Make one end fast to the bow cleat. I'll take the other and try to haul you off." After a mad scramble, a line was found and secured. Dave and Peter took the rest of the rope into the skiff and rowed for the opposite shore, playing out the line as they went. "We'll tie it to the axel on the truck, hang on tight and hope like hell."

They carried what was left of the umbilicus to the truck parked on the boat ramp. The rope was tied to the back of the Chevy pickup and then Dave put the truck in four wheel drive and inched ahead to take up the slack. "They must be a little worried by now," Pete said.

The line came up tight and Dave pressed the gas pedal. "Thank God there's no ice or snow on the ramp," he said.

Pat and I watched a spray of glistening frozen water shower from the rope, squeezing from the line as it narrowed. It sparkled in the twilight, giving the impression of a mini- fireworks display. Dave stopped the forward momentum, caught his breath and then with all the power the duel axels could handle, the truck moved forward. The Coast Guard vessel hesitated then slid off the marsh, rocking back and forth, madly thrashing rail to rail. All hands present and accounted for.

The line was untied from the boat cleat and dropped in the water. The engines on the cutter came to life with a roar. There was a wave of a hand to Peter and Dave signaling that they were on their own power. Goodbye and good luck the wave seemed to say as they motored away from the tiny basin, into the river, out past the jetties, into Cape Cod Bay and home to Provincetown. The four of us squeezed into the truck cab and stared at the disappearing boat. The moon painted a silver glow on the water. I looked at Dave, then Dave and Peter and Pat and I all looked at one another. If there had been anyone in the dunes surrounding the harbor that night they would have heard fits of laughter across the open water.

"That was close." Dave said and we talked over the next move. "We can tackle the one up on the marsh tomorrow, now that we have that hundred fathom coil of line. Do you think we can pull her off Pete?"

"We can give it a try." Their enthusiasm undaunted, "Let's meet here at the parking lot in the morning. That boat won't be going anywhere." Pete said.

"Thanks, Pete" Dave said in a quiet voice.

"Ah, what are friends for, and besides this was the best show in town."

Over the years these two local men have witnessed many storms and a number of wrecks, but this one hit close to home. The next morning we were watching the water make its' way slowly up into the Pamet River via the breakwaters. A beautiful morning, the sun sparkling on the water, it felt downright warm after the night of bitter cold and howling wind. "Things always look better in the daylight," Peter said.

They unloaded the frozen coil of line into the skiff, appearing to have no trouble lifting the heavy pile. "Nice of the boys to donate this rope," Pete commented as they prepared to once again row across the basin, this time to attach the line to the stricken boat and walk the coil back across the marsh. Then using the skiff, take it to the *'Sea Butcher'*.

Dock talk had brought a few local men down to the harbor to see the boat up on the marsh. Pat and I could hear them as we sat in her Volvo with the windows open, heater on.

Our eyes were glued to our heroes who were moving across the marsh with precision steps, holding the coil of rope between them. The audience became vocal, "They'll never get her off from there. Looks like Dave's got his hands full. I can't see any way to bring her back to the basin. She's done for sure, can't see why he'd want to salvage it from the looks of her." What they didn't know was that a plan had been hatched during a practice session on the previous eve.

The men were hiking back, playing out the rope as they went, boots crunching on the frozen grasses. With fewer strokes of the oars, the skiff was alongside the '*Sea Butcher*' in record time. David secured the line to the stern cleats in the form of a triangle, so that the boat would pull from the center. Peter's boat belched black smoke, coughing out any remaining carbon like it was clearing its throat. Pete pushed the throttle down for more power. The line came up tight and then that wild stranded boat, all forty two feet of zebra looking hull, began to move with what could only be described as a graceful glide. The cold working in their favor providing a skating pond, "Keep a strain on the line." Pete yelled in his excitement. The line between boat and boat squeezed as tight as a two inch hawser could get, thinning to half its width. The '*Sea Butcher*' moved forward. That wooden hulk slid across the frozen ice like a skating ballerina from the 'Ice Capades' at Madison Square Garden, her dignity only partially bruised. We heard cracking, crushing, breaking, snapping, then, kerplop. There was a spray of salt water, then splashing and finally the rocking of a floating boat.

Pete pulled the throttle back and swung his boat around, bringing it alongside the rocking and rolling, slowly quieting vessel. A slack tide, a little wind and a rush of adrenaline made hauling in that rope for the last time - a piece of cake. Pete brought the 'Sea Butcher' alongside the new addition to the fleet. That wild thing was secured on another mooring, safe for the moment. The temperature was hovering around freezing and both men were sweating. They boarded her to see what damage was sustained in the drag back to water. Hardly a trickle greeted them when they checked out her bilges. Then a new sound came from inside the boat; the sound of two men whooping, yahooing and laughing.

"That rope kept getting heavier, must have weighed five hundred pounds by the time we got it back to the boat." Peter said.

"Every day brings something new, don't you think, Pete?"

"It's what life's all about," was the reply.

"Bad start, good end," Dave said. A travel lift trailer truck showed up next day on the high tide. Once again the 'Sea Butcher' moved into action, bringing the little boat safely to the ramp for haul out. The forty-two foot hull was carried to her temporary home on Beach Point. The first leg of her journey was complete.

On days when he was not out fishing with Raymond, Dave could be found refurbishing the old wooden boat. Planks in the hull were replaced, seams re-caulked and a new wheelhouse was built. Beginning with a bare hull the foc'sle took shape, a double bunk was added in the forepeak, a couch on the right (starboard) and a table with benches on the port side, then a sink and a toilet, a gimbaled stove and a camping cooler for refrigeration completed the living space. A gift came to us from Captain Justin Avellar, owner and captain of the '*Hindu*' in the form of a most needed engine, free and it would get us where we needed to go.

We were taking a moment's rest on a pleasant day in spring, sitting on the rail at the stern of our almost completed fishing boat with Peter and Pat, when Pat asked, "I'm wondering, what are you going to name this boat?" She said, "She's a wild thing and it's spring, why not call her 'Wildflower'." All four of us were bobbing our heads up and down. The name stuck.

CHAPTER 3

The Romance Leaves When You Cast Off the Lines

We received our first fishing permit from the state of Massachusetts just a few months after our son Jackson was born in 1971. The weather warmed and a special fishing boat was launched at the Pamet Harbor. We were surrounded by new life, good friends and the dunes of the cape. I poured champagne over the bow, said a little prayer and watched as the boat once again touched water. The *'Wildflower's'* engine roared at the turn of the key. Dave pushed the throttle forward and maneuvered out past the jetties into Cape Cod Bay, taking the boat to her new home at MacMillan Wharf in Provincetown.

Most of the boats that made up the Provincetown fleet were bigger than our day boat, but Dave and I were comfortable with what we had. We felt we could trust the *'Wildflower'*, we knew her from top to bottom. I would never be afraid to sleep onboard and Dave knew she'd catch fish, scallops, lobsters and many other varieties of seafood. We were looking forward to a bright future.

Dave fished every day, but I was a part-time fisher-folk, staying home when I was needed as mom. There were two wonderful grandmas to keep an eye on our growing son — so I began fishing with Dave whenever I could. We rotated between our small apartment and the boat, our little family slept both on land and on the water. Our son Jackson was one year old when Ralph Andrews, who owned and captained the 'Petrel' stopped Dave on the wharf. Ralph bought a steel hulled boat after he'd returned from fishing in the Bering Sea off Alaska. He had fished with his father on the *Captain Bill* growing up in Provincetown. The two men had known each other all their lives. He told Dave about a bed of sea scallops being worked to the east of Chatham, MA. He said, "Follow me down to the scallop grounds. I'll put you right on them."

Dave was raring to go. I decided to make this trip because I wanted the adventure and I could help with the cutting and opening of the scallops, besides our mothers were vying to help with our son's care. We left with the tide at midnight, watching the running lights of the 'Petrel' for four hours. It was a calm, starry night when we left the harbor. With not much to see, I climbed into the bunk and slept fitfully. When I awoke I experienced an eerie nautical twilight. I was standing next to Dave as blackness turned to grey. I felt I was flying inside a cloud unable to see beyond the bow. We had moved into a fog bank.

Ralph and Dave kept up a conversation on the CB radio during the trip. The 'Petrel' was equipped with radar, we were not. Ralph could see our blip on his screen. He said, "Set out anywhere, Dave, you're right on them. Keep the tow short, no more than fifteen minutes."

Over went the rake, a nine foot massive hunk of iron made up of iron rings hanging from a triangular shaped iron frame. I could hear the chains and iron rings tinkling like wind chimes as the seven-hundred pounds hung in the air. The rake is attached to the boat with a thick woven metal wire that runs to a hydraulic winch. The wire goes through a series of blocks that allow it to be steered onto the winch drum. The machine squeaks, groans and if it needs greasing, it shrieks so loud it sounds like a banshee being strangled. The rig needs to turn fast because hundreds of feet of wire have to be let out and off the boat in order for the rake to touch the bottom without flipping over. The sooner you get that rake back out and fishing, the sooner you haul back. The sooner the scallops are on deck, the sooner you get to go home.

When the rake came up after the first tow it was so full of sea scallops that they were falling out the top. We began jumping for joy, shouting into the colorless world of fog. Dave yelled out, "Get the rake back over." He was pumped and it didn't matter that he'd been up all night. We had never seen anything like this. Scalloping in Cape Cod Bay just didn't compare. Inside the bay you dig through piles of sand, mud, sand-dollars, monkey-dung and starfish. Here tow after tow proved to be as exciting as the first, just pure unopened shells. We were shoveling scallops into the foc'sle and heaping them in the stern. Around ten o'clock the fog lifted and -holy smoke- we were surrounded by large boats out of New

Bedford, Gloucester, New Jersey, Rhode Island and Maine. Everyone knew we were there, but we didn't know they were. Our next purchase would be a Raytheon Radar system.

The '*Wildflower*' sat in the water like a sea gull, but my poor stomach was floating six feet over my head and between tows I was puking over the side. I begged Dave to throw me overboard. "Just one more tow honey then I'll take you home," he tried to be conciliatory, but he just wanted to keep fishing. Sea sickness is like no other type of illness. Only the thought of dying keeps you going. The head goes into a cloud of headache and a jelly- like feeling comes over you. The stomach churns and you cannot control anything. Then weakness sets in and the lack of strength is frightening. Fear mingles with sweat and then you puke. Eventually your head gets accustomed to motion and after you are able to keep down saltines and water, you know you'll survive.

The swells began to subsided and we were underway heading north with the changing tide. Having run out of room on deck, there was no choice but to leave the big boats and the big pile of sea scallops behind. We were happy with our share. We didn't have an autopilot to steer for us, so Dave tied the wheel while we cut open the scallops. I sat on top of the pile, a seat of shells and began shucking the inedible parts into the sea to be devoured by the sea gulls, our constant companions. We shoveled and pushed sea scallops around the deck so that we could get as close to the rail as possible.

The guts and shells had to go overboard and with as little effort as possible. Dave nailed a wooden box to the rail to act as a table because we knew it would take hours of repetitious cutting to finish the load. Inside the box a stainless steel bowl sat waiting to accept the meats. When opening a sea scallop a peculiar knife is used - wide at the tip, narrow mid-blade then wide again. Most cutters have their own special knife with the handle wrapped in black electrical tape to fit the shape of their palm. You can usually spot an enlarged muscle just above the wrist near the thumb on the guys who have been at it awhile. This muscle develops over time from that repetitive movement.

The idea is to scrape the meat off the top shell, flick the guts and shell over the side, then cut the muscle into the stainless bucket. As one becomes good at it, opening a sea scallop can be done in one movement of the wrist. A clean swift motion: blade in, scrape, blade out, flip the shell while holding guts to the top; another quick motion of the wrist and plop goes the top shell along with the rim, stomach and gonads, onto the surface of the water. On and on it goes while the gulls wait and watch from their invisible perch in the sky. They swoop down and snatch up the remains, sometimes before the waste hits the water. There's a sweet smell in the air, which I'm sure the birds must sense from miles away. How else could they just appear out of nowhere, miles from shore and no land on the horizon? We fed the gulls and the ocean fed us; it seemed like a good balance.

On the way back to port Dave placed a tarp over the mollusks, wetting them periodically with cold sea water. We opened the bivalves as fast as we could. We then washed them in salt water, poured them into clean white muslin bags and then ice was shoveled on top, keeping them fresh but not frozen. How sweet they are, because they are on restaurant tables within hours.

We hadn't made much of a dent in the pile by the time we came around Long Point and entered Provincetown Harbor, so Dave went ashore to phone for help. The only cutters he could find were Marie Santos, the 60 year old wife of Captain 'Cutty' Santos and David's mother, Juliana, who was talked into coming along by Marie. Marie and her husband had worked their own fishing boat, the *'Cutty's Ark'* for many years, but it was sold in the 1960's because of the captain's health problems. "I'm still willing and able to wield a shucking knife," Marie told us.

The boat was on a mooring in the harbor instead of tied to the wharf, so the women were brought out to the *'Wildflower'* using a small skiff. The scallop debris would be eaten by fish, crabs and waterfowl. Dave's mom was a land-lubber and we knew this was a treat for all of us. It was the perfect day, warm with a gentle breeze. The ladies were tickled pink to be helping out. We had to cut, wash, bag and ice the scallops waiting in a large mound at the stern. We went straight to work. Cold sea water ran over the decks continuously. It pruned up our hands and without trying, we were wet from head to toe. The hot sun warmed us as the cold water cooled us.

There was money to be made and this was not a social visit. During the three hours standing at the rail we talked and laughed about by-gone times. "We all come from families of fishermen." Marie said. "David's father and grandfather fished with my husband and his family many years ago." These women had shared a time I could only read about, they spoke of people I could never meet, yet I felt a kinship to them like being joined to their families through the love of fishing and the sea. Marie told about when she was growing up when no one owned a car and sea scallops were a rarity. Mussels were considered the poor man's food and many families were very poor, living from the fish brought to town each day and given away to anyone who asked. "And we could always pick a bucket of muscles from the rocks at low tide," Marie said. "There were days when my family had nothing else to eat. Maybe that's why I don't eat mussels, but I love scallops." She had fished alongside her husband for years. "Then the doctor told him he shouldn't go out fishing because of his heart, so he stopped going and we sold the boat. He misses it terribly."

"I don't eat sea scallops, I'm allergic." I told them, "But I love mussels." We proceeded to cut out ten more bags. The smiling was all the pay they needed, but they took home enough sweet meats to cook for supper. We had twenty-two bags, each bag held forty pounds. We were paid $2.50 a pound, for a total of $2200. Not bad for eighteen hours of work.

Exhausted, I slept soundly and was up with our son at dawn the next morning. Dave knew there was money to be made so he drove to Hyannis and bought a new radar system to be installed the following week. I thought I'd have a couple of days off, but Dave was keyed up and ready to go again. We hoped to do as well or better than the first trip. This time Dave and I had help. Another good friend and very experienced fisherman, Richard Dickey went along to give us a hand. He and David had been friends for many years and we valued any pointers he could give us.

This trip proved to be as plentiful. We were enthralled by the money we could make and this led to our learning a new lesson. The captain wanted just one more tow, it was like finding gold, difficult to stop and float away. We had ten bags on ice and were cutting more bivalves on the way home when we ran out of fuel. All three of us scanned the horizon for any fishing boat heading up the coast to give us a tow, but there were none. Dave had to call the Coast Guard to request assistance. We radioed our position, just east of the Highland Lighthouse, a description of the boat and the number of persons on board. We were not in any immediate danger, it was calm enough and we were far enough off shore not to worry about being stranded on the beach - so we would have to wait until the Coast Guard could get to us. With Richard cutting scallops faster than either Dave or me, twenty bags were on ice before we knew it. Then we waited and waited. We doze and waited. I fried scallops and potatoes for the men, I ate peanut butter sandwiches and we continued watching, dozing and waiting. There wasn't much conversation. We drifted miles. No loran bearings to give anyone, just radio conversation estimating our position.

I didn't like feeling so alone but I was certain that nothing bad would happen to us. After six hours, at twilight, just before darkness enveloped us, there they were - a big white boat with orange strip across the bow. I could feel the relief to my bones. They gave us a tow back to Provincetown Harbor while I wondered if it was the same crew that we had rescued two winters before in Pamet Harbor. Thanks to the U.S. Coast Guard and thanks to the God who watches out for fools and fishermen we were home planning the next trip that evening.

I learned many lessons while learning to fish. The rules are there for a reason. "If you look up at the sky or wharf or rigging, keep your mouth shut - never leave a hatch turned upside down and never, ever, question the captain." As Dave always tells me, "The romance leaves when you cast off the lines. We began making three or four trips a week to the scallop grounds. I learned quickly that I needed to rest between trips. The work-hours were long. If we had to cut and open the scallops by ourselves, it was twice the work, but more money in the bank. Dave hired crewmen when he could, finding help was difficult. Men that loved fishing were already doing it. There were so many boats bringing in scallops that men were jumping at the chance to make a week's pay.

Bruce turned up at the right time, looking for work, a local young man. He made a number of trips with us during the first summer; he even brought along his girlfriend on a run down the back of the Highlands. We were fortunate to have good calm weather. Four hours to the scallop grounds, load up the boat and cut as fast as we could, load up again and cut as much as the boat would hold and cut more on the way back. We paid him the going rate of ten dollars for every ten quart bucket he shucked, but his girlfriend didn't know how to cut scallops and just came along for the ride. By the time we entered port we were finished and cleaning up, ready to unload.

The scallops, purchased by Seafood Packers, were making their way skyward in wooden boxes. It was low tide and Bruce was looking up to the platform about sixteen feet above his head. It's a good idea to keep an eye on what is going on around you, especially since a box weighs about one hundred pounds. Bruce is one of those guys who, when he stretches his head backwards, his mouth automatically opens. I don't believe a seagull could have had Bruce in mind when it made the perfect shot. Guano landed right in his open boca! He was spitting, coughing and gagging. Then he grabbed the deck hose and stuck it in his mouth. The heavy stream of salt water did the trick. I told him I was sorry for laughing, but then he began laughing. Thanks to Bruce I learned to keep my mouth closed on the boat looking up from the deck and always wear a hat, you never know where the shit will land.

"The captain is always right, don't ask questions, and do as you're told." Dave can be gruff. He's patient with me most of the time, but I ask a lot of questions and it can get on his nerves: "Why did you do it that way, or what if you did that this way?" Dave and I would begin to argue. I'd scream at him, "I quit!" Then it would get quiet on deck. The purr of the engine and the screeching gulls was all that could be heard. We did not talk for an hour, and then we'd both go on like nothing had happened. I'd do my job picking up scallops, hooking up the rake and cut scallops into the bucket. Then I would sit on the rail in my oil gear looking at nothing, wondering what I was doing there. I couldn't believe that all this came so naturally to him; that he didn't have to think about what he did, he just did what was needed and he didn't need to question himself when it came to being on the water. I did. Fishing and boats are a strange world to me, and a struggle because I am always wondering at the mystery of it all. I think I quit about a dozen times that first summer, but he always took me back and I learned it isn't necessary to question the captain, he is always right.

What I was doing there was working hard at something I knew almost nothing about. But you couldn't beat the view. I'd watch the sky, the water, and the birds and a feeling of peacefulness that I didn't encounter on land, inspired me to see beyond myself. The roar of the engine didn't matter. The motion of the boat lulls you. The best times for me were spent fishing in Cape Cod Bay digging through piles of sand, specks of fish tails sticking out, a lobster grabbing the fin of a flounder, colorful star fish lying on the sand. The deck became my garden, and the mud and sand, my earth. On some hot summer days Mother Nature would reward us with the most surprising things; like the time we were fifteen miles offshore, fishing the Stellwagen Bank, standing at the rail cutting scallops when out of the blue small yellow birds appeared. They began eating all the flies they could find, and on hot summer days there are usually a few to be had, even way out there. The small migrating birds were stopping to eat and rest. They are a special sight, spots of the brightest yellow and white against the greens and blues of sea and sky. Then suddenly they are gone, off to the horizon.

When the temperature gets up over 80 degrees even with a sea breeze it feels hot. Then I stand under the deck hose to cool off. Every boat has one. It pumps water onto the deck from the sea and is used for washing and cleaning fish, scallops, the boat or us. The water leaves you cooler, but as the air dries you a thin coating of salt can make your skin itch just slightly. It tastes remarkably good and as long as you don't lick too much of it, I suppose it's not bad for you. Fresh water is very precious on a boat and we learned to keep a sun-shower bag on the roof of the wheel house. The sun heats the water in the black plastic bag. When there is just the two of us on the boat I'd strip down to my birthday suit to rinse off. "Let me know if you see any boats coming this way," I ask. Dave laughs and tells me to look around. There is not a boat or plane or bird to be seen but that doesn't stop me from feeling naked.

Once the scallops are cleaned, bagged and iced, we'd get naked and rinse off with hot fresh water. This afternoon treat gives us the energy to finish the day; sell the product and grab a bite to eat before falling into the bunk to start fresh at four in the a.m. The tank hidden under the forward bunk holds the water we use for cooking and cleaning up before bed if we are staying on board — many nights are spent at home on land but many more are spent on board the 'Wildflower'. We are constantly reminded of how valuable fresh water is. I learned to wash up our supper dishes with less than a quart of fresh water, using a spray bottle and a tiny bit of soap. How's that for conservation?

It is wise to keep a lookout when taking a shower on deck. One afternoon Dave and I were scalloping on top of the Middle Bank when out of nowhere a small open skiff with an outboard engine appeared alongside us. There were two men with a cooler and a couple of fishing poles. One of the men asked, "Which way to Provincetown?"

David and I looked at them in amazement. "Do you fellows have a compass?" Dave asked. They both moved their heads from side to side. They didn't tie to us just wanted the directions, like at a gas station on the interstate. Dave pointed in the general direction they needed to go and said, "Keep a lookout for the monument. It stands out above the dunes." The men nodded their heads and zipped away toward the unseen land.

"See," I said to Dave. "What if I'd been taking a shower? You never know who might drop in."

The sea scallops that come from Cape Cod Bay are the biggest you'll ever see; two meats can fill a coffee cup. Tencount, they're called - ten to a pound - the kind that brings top dollars and they are not found anywhere else in the world. They are bigger than the scallops we caught in the Atlantic Ocean and are entirely different from bay scallops. The shells measure six to nine inches across. To me the shells are as beautiful as the meats. When our son, Jackson was seven years old he was painting pictures inside the shells, so I'd save as many shells as I could carry home. Dave, Jackson and I lived aboard the '*Wildflower*' whenever we could. Jackson stayed with his grandparents on Beach Point or at our apartment in the center of town with my mom who came frequently to visit. Having our family living close made all the difference, I don't think I'd have gone fishing if we did not have the help of our families. We also had help from our friends.

Captain Justin Avellar gave us the engine for our boat and he gave us a berth on his float at MacMillan Wharf, across from his schooner '*Hindu*'. Captain Avellar was a retired Merchant Marine Seaman and a Boston Harbor Pilot before coming to Provincetown. Dave and Captain Avellar became fast friends over the years. In exchange for helping with things the '*Hindu*' couldn't do like setting up and taking down the float in the spring and fall, Dave checked moorings and went along as crew when Captain Avellar took the '*Hindu*' to Falmouth for winter berthing.

The two men could sometimes be seen sitting on the wooden curb in front of the '*Hindu*'s' booth on MacMillan Wharf. The old salt's grey hair peeked out from under the Portuguese fisherman's hat. Justin would take the ever present pipe from his mouth and say "Look at that girl. You can see the cheeks of her ass. I wouldn't let my daughters out of the house dressed like that." They'd laugh like hell while they talked about the weather, boats and tourists. We could always tell when Justin was on the wharf by the sweet scent of his Prince Albert tobacco that floated in the air. I can still hear Justin's gravelly voice giving orders to his crew. The boat's signal horn would sound three short blasts, then Justin growled out orders "Let go the bow line, stern line. Let go the spring line." Captain Avellar could sail the *'Hindu'* with his eyes closed. He'd pull his watch from his pocket and look at the compass and say, "its always foggy so you'd better know where you are at all times." When he was eighty-five years old, Justin had cataract surgery. Afterward he'd joke about sailing blind. He taught me to love to sail, to not be afraid to use the wind and I'll love him always for that gift.

The years that the *'Wildflower'* tied next to the *'Hindu'* were filled with new experiences, sunrises on the bay, the nautical twilight of dawn and the passions of youth. I learned about fishing and what it took to be a fisherman's wife. We had to earn our way, learning overcoming new challenges as we went.

The changing of seasons usually means changing gear. In the fall I went back to work at the school and we moved back to our rental on shore. The fall is the time to drag out the flat-net. This is a small, lightweight net with a tickler chain along the bottom and a few balls along the head rope to keep her open. Fish would be traveling south or out to deeper water for winter so getting out during September, October and November could mean a financially comfortable winter. The net always needs to be checked before it goes onto the boat. Dave stretches it out in the driveway, sewing any holes in the mesh with twine; using a technique similar to macramé. I look out my kitchen window and watch him sitting on an overturned bucket with mending needle in hand. He learned to mend a net the same way as most fishermen do, by watching others then practicing. When he was ten years old his neighbor showed him how to thread the needles. The Salvador family had Provincetown draggers tied to the town wharf for as long as anyone could remember and sons to run them. They built nets in their basement and the local kids would sometimes get to hang out there. Nets need sewing on a regular basis. Sometimes it's just a few holes that need repair and sometimes it's a whole section, taking days to mend. One small hole can mean many fish will be lost. Today the regulated size of the mesh is 6 inches and is one of the best regulations imposed for protecting juvenile fish. Small fish swim through the holes, or meshes in the net. There are different nets for the different types of fishing but for the highly regulated flat fish, a six inch mesh works well and has helped to create the way to sustainability in fishing.

Building or repairing nets is part of the job. Nets tear easily. "The bottom has teeth," Dave says. Many hours are spent bent over a net laid out in the yard. The mending twine is harsh on the fingers because gloves can't be used; they just get in the way. Sewing with bear hands can cause cuts and small tears to the skin. The hands of a fisherman are tough, hard, calloused from use, unprotected from the elements. The bones get stiff and slow because of the damp and wet. They can peel, crack and the sun can do damage, but the hands of my fisherman are strong, warm and gentle.

As I watch from the kitchen window I wonder how much repair will be needed this year. The net has been lying on the ground for a year. Keeping a spare net in the yard always makes sense, they wear out, tear up and are occasionally are pulled from the boat by a wreck or other obstruction. Dave has had experience with all three. With a cup of tea for Dave, I step into the yard. "How does it look?"

"Not so bad this time." Dave said. "I'll replace the head rope and mend any holes. I can attach this new section of twine if I have to." He held a red handled knife that glistened in the sunlight. I fill the needles with the twine while he sips the hot tea. The sun disintegrates the twine, so it is kept covered when not used, but then the cover attracts mice and they eat the twine, so mending the net is just another part of the business. For whatever reason, the time spent on net mending is a double expense - Dave can't be out catching fish and the twine is expensive, but for me watching Dave mending a net, home in our yard, warms my heart. He learned to fish beside family and friends, by observing and helping, but trial and error gave him experience. I don't believe there is a school that can teach you to fish. If you have the incentive, the health, a little know-how and the money - then maybe, you will also have a certain gene that calls you to the sea.

Our son Jackson learned at an early age how to operate equipment, how to handle the fish, how to pilot a skiff and how to maneuver it in the water. Jackson seemed to absorb the waterman's life by osmosis. At the age of nine he began running errands for yachts visiting our harbor. Dave gave him the use of a sixteen foot wooden boat with a small outboard motor. We watched him from the deck of the '*Wildflower*' as he zipped around the moorings stopping at a number of sailboats

53

anchored in the harbor, like giving your son a dirt bike to wheel around the yard. He was making gas money for the skiff, learning and having fun until the weekend of Fourth-of-July when the harbor filled with sailboats. During that holiday weekend he made $300 and since he was only nine years old we knew he had to start a savings account, a boy could get hurt with that kind of money. He gave up on the business of picking up garbage and making deliveries to yachts when his earning fell back to less than $25.00 for the week. Summer fun was calling and his experiences were expanding.

We didn't spend all of our time on the boat, but Jackson and I loved being on board in the summer. I'd cook meals, clean fish and daydream, but it is never boring on the boat, Jackson would fish with a hook and line when we were towing, he'd play with the deck hose, keep a lookout for whales, and find treasures among the piles of bottom debris brought to the deck. We began collecting old bottles, and nautical oddities to bring home from the sea. On more than one occasion Dave would stop the boat in the middle of the bay and Jackson and I would go swimming while Dave kept a lookout for us. "Come on in," I yell at the captain.

His answer, "I like being on top of the water, not in it."

One day after fishing for the day in Cape Cod Bay, David brought the *'Wildflower'* alongside the *'Peter & Linda'*- a sixty foot Provincetown dragger- to wait for our turn to unload. Captain Saraphine Codinha was a top earner in the fishing fleet and highly respected among the locals. He was unloading ten thousand pounds of mixed fish on this afternoon with one hundred boxes stacked in rows across the deck. They seemed to tower above the '*Wildflower*'. Captain Codinha, built like a long-shore-men, stepped from his wheelhouse and spoke to Dave in a fatherly way, "You've done a nice job with that little boat," he said.

Dave watched the dragger unload then looked at his own small catch of a thousand pounds and I could almost feel his envy. "It must feel good to have a catch like that on deck," Dave answered.

The old man nodded his head and replied, "Maybe, you'll do the same someday."

The fish, sea scallops and the lobsters that we caught fed family, friends, townsfolk and people we will never meet. We caught enough to keep us comfortably afloat and I managed to save. "I don't need much," I'd tell Dave.

"When the bank account gets low - I'll go out and make a withdrawal from Cape Cod Bay and Trust," was his reply. Dave fished ten months of the year, the other two being too stormy to be economical or safe, but he is always yearning to be out there catching fish. Each year by the end of December the '*Wildflower*' was on stanchions in the yard. "Boats need upkeep. We'll haul her out and put her back as soon as possible in spring. Boats are better off in the water; they lose their shape after sitting out too long. It's called 'hogging'. If a boat hogs, it's beginning to bulge in places she shouldn't, like a middle aged matron with not enough exercise," Dave said. He might have been hinting that I was putting on weight, but I doubt it because he'd come right out and tell me what he thought and in no uncertain terms.

When spring comes to the lower cape, the boat goes back to work. Dave will use the scallop rake for a while then change to sea clams, lobster and flatfish as the seasons change. The weather in spring is precarious and can keep the boats tied to the wharf for days and weeks at a time, so it is a blessing to be able to fish close to home and in the lee. For a day-boat like the '*Wildflower*' it was a necessity. At the first sign of summer warmth fish begin to move and return, and so the rake would be exchanged for a net. Our nets are called a three-quarter net, light enough to be towed at just the right speed and heavy enough to easily catch a thousand pounds a day when pulled by our small boat. We bought our first net from the Levin family in Fairhaven in 1971 and we have been back to their shop a thousand times since.

For almost ten years David worked the '*Wildflower*', spending many hours out upon the ocean. The business prospered, allowing us to buy a new truck and then my dream came true. We bought our own home. Our lives were just a little off the main stream; quiet and removed from the rest of the world, but no different than any working family, making payments and hoping for a better life and then one day I told David we were going to have our second child, and he said to me "The '*Wildflower*' is not big enough."

And I thought — "Now, where have I heard that before?

CHAPTER 4

F/V Richard & Arnold

For most of the year-round population a ride down the town wharf is integrated into the day. We go to look at the boats, the wharfs and harbor. During the winter months while our 'Wildflower" was hauled out of the water, fifty or sixty boats were still making a living bringing in Whiting, Codfish, Sea Scallops and a variety of other edible products from the sea. Although it was a cold February day, the sparkling sun on the water held the promise of spring. Dave stopped the truck at the end of the pier and said, "See that boat over there? I hear it's for sale and I think we should buy it."

He sat behind the wheel of his GMC pickup truck while I held our newborn baby Robert in my arms. In-between us our ten-year old son, Jackson leaned closer to the windshield to stare out at the fishing boats tied 3 and 4 abreast to the pier. "The black one with the yellow boot-top," Dave had read my thoughts.

The 'Wildflower' was hauled out waiting for warmer weather. Fishing had provided us with enough income to buy a house and things were looking up. We had discussed the possibility of a larger fishing boat many times during the past few years and I think we were both prepared for a change. Our ten year old knew right away which boat dad was talking about, "The *Richard & Arnold*?" Jackson read the name out loud. "Can I go fishing with you?" he asked. Jackson had experienced the ocean in its many forms. This youngster was ready for fishing.

Dad smiled and said, "Well, thanks son, but you've got to go to school, maybe this summer, we'll see." He went on to explain, "The boat was built in Fairhaven, Massachusetts by Casey Boat Building Co. in 1924 and began fishing in 1927. She's 52 feet on the waterline and 60 feet overall with a beam of 15 feet. She draws 7 feet, a deep keel for such a small boat, but that's what makes her seaworthy." I could hear the excitement beginning to grow.

What I saw was a Provincetown dragger. The boat had a sleek, polished look. With a small grey wheel house situated toward the stern she's known as an 'Eastern-rigged' dragger. I could just make out her name on the bow, 'F/V Richard & Arnold', followed by a set of numbers. "This is a big step," Inside I was filled with jitters. "If you think you can handle it, I'm with you 100%." It appeared the decision was made. We celebrated with a dinner at a local Chinese Restaurant. At the end of the meal my fortune cookie said, "Hold on to his shirt tail" and Dave's said, "You will succeed beyond your wildest dreams." Well, how could we not be excited about life?

We signed the ownership papers, the loan papers, the documentation papers and the fishing-license papers two months later at the lawyer's office in New Bedford in 1982. As we were leaving, paperwork in hand, we were told about a man named Charlie Westgate who had worked for Casey's boatyard when our fishing boat was built. We had to meet this man so we took a detour on the way home.

He was sitting in an armchair looking all of his ninety years, but his blue eyes twinkled with life. He was glad to hear about the *'Richard & Arnold'*. "One of Casey's finest," he told us. "Fairhaven in those days built many a vessel; hardly any have survived this long. We built them to last, but you know how it is out there on the water." He added, "With a little love she'll last your lifetime too." He remembered Casey's boat yard that ran for a city block, from their railway along the waterfront to the beginning of the residential area. "The buildings were long, low and filled with every sort of ship building tool and material imaginable." He smiled, and then his face became serious. "There was a big fire in 1956, a lot of the equipment was lost and all of Casey's records and ship designs. Casey built a few with John Alden. We had French shipbuilders who had somehow found their way to New Bedford at the turn of the century. The *'Richard & Arnold'* has quite a history."

There was no stopping the old man, "If I remember right that boat was commissioned by Dutch Shultz, the gangster. He was going to run rum with it during prohibition in the 1920's or at least that was the yard gossip. I don't know why, but Dutch Shultz never came to get it. She sat in a barn for a number of years before Frank Parson brought the boat to Provincetown for fishing." he chuckled at his memories.

"She's a good sea boat. Fast, too. That's the way Casey built them. Boats meant to last." We thanked him for his time. "Good fishing," were his last words as we left him with his memories, sitting in his easy chair.

Over the years we have had visits and welcomes from people who show up at the dock and tell us how they remembered her. "I remember when" is how they begin. "She's named for Frank Parson's two sons. The *Richard & Arnold* was run by Frank and his brother Henry, bringing in more fish than anyone else, on any given day, high-liners they were called. The *Richard & Arnold* landed millions of pounds of fish that was delivered to markets in Gloucester, Boston and New Bedford as well as Provincetown. One day not long after we bought her Dave and I met Captain Parson on MacMillan Wharf and he told us that during World War II the *Richard & Arnold* fished but also watched the coast for intruders and unusual activity, all fishing boats were documented and expected to keep a sharp lookout during the war. "She never saw an enemy, just lots of fish." Captain Parson smiled and said, "Good luck."

He told us that the Parson family sold the boat to Charley Bennett with partner Donald Walwer when they began buying fish instead of catching it. Charley bought out Donald and then hired Anthony Thomas to captain her. After a number of years, Alfred Silva bought the vessel as a second fishing boat to work with his family. The fishing tradition continued when she was sold again to Garren and Holway. They hired a captain who was the grandson of Anthony Thomas, also named Anthony Thomas. Then along came Dave with his wife and family. For the past eighty years she has remained a Provincetown boat. The *'Richard & Arnold'* has a history to be proud of and we knew the boat was good at what it did.

It was a time of expansion for us. David had been fishing and scalloping his pocket dragger. He'd done well, learned a lot, but the family and the business were growing and so we weighed the pros and cons of a bigger boat. The *"Wildflower"* could be hauled out of the water and carried on a trailer over land to be deposited in a field. This not only was cheaper but Dave could work on improvements while the boat was in the yard.

We also had the option of going much bigger - with one of the new offshore steel trawlers, but I knew what that would mean. Dave would be gone for weeks at a time because the bigger the boat, the more it can hold, the longer the boat had to stay out and the more we would have to pay back to the bank. "The *'Richard & Arnold'* is a town boat," I said. "She belongs here with the rest of the Provincetown fleet. I like her lines. I'm confident you can make money with it."

"The *'Richard & Arnold'* carries more fish, stays out twenty-four hours if the fish are there." Dave knew it was a good move. "There's the railway every year - a big expense," Dave nodded to me. "Her wooden hull needs yearly maintenance and I'm going to need to make it safer. It goes without saying that the boat requires the attention of a mistress." Of course I didn't need much convincing.

The *'Wildflower'* was sold and taken away on a trailer. We were excited about the new boat, it felt like a natural progression. It was bittersweet for me, sorry about seeing our

'Wildflower' leave, but looking forward to the future. Dave on the other hand is practical and not as sentimental. "They say the best days of owning a boat are the day you buy it and the day you sell it," Dave said. The 'Wildflower' was a fine little ship that carried us into the fishing business and it will never be forgotten - for all the lessons learned, the fish, scallops and lobsters caught and for the money earned, but it was time to move on.

We borrowed $50,000 to make the 'Richard & Arnold' ours, a big debt on top of our house mortgage. It put pressure on us to make more money so that we could pay the bank. We knew it was possible to make a good day's pay if you put in the time and effort, the 'Wildflower' had taught us that. The fish were there. My role changed from chief cook / deck hand to homemaker / landlubber. My days of fishing were coming to an end. This was serious fishing and Dave would hire crewmen. He didn't have time to coddle me and I was needed on shore with two growing boys. I had my job at the school and would keep the home fires burning.

Dave had plans, "I'm going to rig her for dragging — with some changes. I'll also be able to go scalloping when we need to." Before we bought the boat, it had been rigged the old fashion way: using the mast with a block and tackle and one winch to lift the net and fish over the side. Dave had seen the new rigs on the boats in Fairhaven and New Bedford. The practicalities of hydraulics, the mechanics of pumps and motors; these Dave understood. The path was clear; the boat would be rigged so that he could fish safely when alone or with crewman. Whatever fish there would be in the net would come up and over the stern. Plans included a net reel to operate on hydraulics. "I'll have to spend some money to get the motor and pumps and hoses and special fittings, but this is the way to go," Dave said.

His enthusiasm was infectious as the plan developed. Help came from DEME Winches in Maine and from Harbor Hydraulics in Fairhaven, MA. The 'Richard & Arnold' was turning out to be an old, but modern, inshore dragger and the captain was turning out to be a salty dog. Anyone can call themselves a fisherman, but experience, I have heard, is the best of all instructors. It takes more than just throwing a net off the stern and dragging it around. The net can be full or empty, or worse, a net can become entangled. A fisherman needs to know how to set the net for different species of fish. He needs to know the boat speed over the bottom, the weight of the doors, depth of the water, the direction of the tide, and the time of the year. Some of the knowledge of fishing can come from a book, but takes experience to bring it together. Let's not forget the fact that fish have tails. They swim out of the way when they feel the vibration of a net across the bottom or they are pushed in front of the mouth of the net, away from the wake of it, and they swim through the holes of the 6 inch mesh. Not even a 1/10 of the fish in any given area are caught using our type of dragging. Perhaps this is why the dragger-men of Provincetown have been able to sustain their fishery for almost a hundred years.

Having a practical sense of the laws of physics and knowing what's on the bottom are important in fishing. Where the wrecks are, where the big rocks are, how fast to tow and how to get huge bags aboard, lifting thousands of pounds over the rail without rolling the boat over, the conditions of the sea are part of the knowledge needed to keep a fishing boat working well. Hopefully Dave will always be able to tell when there is something in the net. He'll feel a change in the motion or feel the wire jump or just have a gut feeling and he holler out, "Haul Back! Let's see what we have."

First get the net up to the rail and if there is something unwanted in it, like a telephone pole, a couple of ghost lobster pots, or a huge boulder, anything like that can take all the fun out of fishing. Unwanted debris can rip up the net. Or sometimes Dave will have to cut open a net to remove flotsam and jetsam. He has to remove the items and sown the net back together before he can set the net back over and any number of things can end a fishing trip. A broker is a trip that either costs you or you break even - wasting just your time. Unwanted objects get caught and then it's a matter of getting them out of the net without damaging the boat.

If the debris is large, a timber, or a tree or one time it was the wing of a small airplane, then it will need to be tied with a strong rope to keep it from striking the boat, then winching it aboard so that it can be cut out of the net. Using ropes and tackles, the objective is to get the debris to fall back into the depths without touching the side of the boat. He'll have to cut the net open to remove the big pain in the butt object and it can end the fishing trip by leaving too large a hole to fix on deck.

On other occasions Dave has brought up an empty net. The pit of his stomach gets that sinking feeling. "Lost the whole tow, one step backward," he tells me, "And all because the knot at the end of the bag came untied." So knowing the proper knot to tie under the bag, so that it opens easily yet keeps the fish inside, is another piece of the fishing equation. But, when the net is balanced, has the right amount of wire out, and the doors come up shining, on a day when the seas are less than three feet- then it's all worth the effort. There is always that hope that the net will fill with fish and the boat will hold a day's pay. No matter what kind of day it's been, Dave will return home with a smile on his face for me and the boys.

A good catch of flounder and yellowtail that migrate in the spring and fall has helped many small fishing businesses in Provincetown stay afloat. The 'Richard & Arnold' was able to hire some of the best crews a captain could ask for. One night in November the wind began picking up from the east. Peter Morris and Dave were working the deck. "We'll bring in the net and doors, not much fish anyway." Dave felt it was time to move. The seas were building with swells over seven feet. "Too rough to keep the net down, we'd better head in." Dave brought the boat north, rounding the tip of Race Point while Peter picked up and cleaned the fish that lay on the deck and then put the boxes in the fish hold. By the time they reached Race Point it was blowing a full gale from the East. "Peter," Dave yelled from the wheelhouse, "Nail down the fish hatch, we'll be taking water over the bow until we get round Wood End."

Close to shore can be a dangerous place. There are sandbars that have caught the keel of many a vessel. In his yellow oil gear, dripping wet, Peter stepped into the wheelhouse to get out of the salt spray as the boat pounded her way into the seas. "Nasty out there," Peter looked through the windshield, "It is my understanding that there are shipwrecks lying end to end across the bottom from here to Nauset Inlet." David stares into the radar machine looking for any blip that might be another ship. There were none. Peter braces himself sideways against the door as they rolled with the seas. The *'Richard & Arnold'* slowly made its way around the outer cape.

They were approaching Wood End Lighthouse when Dave asked, "What say we give it a try in the lee of the Truro hills?"

Peter was all for it, "Whatever you say, Cap." They headed inside the Bay, toward the highlands of Truro while the wind howled over their heads at fifty knots. Other boats had the same idea and were already there. The *'Charlotte G'* with Captain Henry Souza and Chris King's *'Second Effort'* were towing while the storm raged. Around one o'clock that morning the eighty-foot fishing boat, the *'MARU'* appeared in the bay. Henry and Chris were on the radio to each other and there was anger in their voices. "A big boat like that one will clean out a small area like this in one day," Henry bellowed over the radio. "He'll take all the fish, his catch could support our whole fleet for a week," Henry hollered. Anyone who had a radio turned on could hear the conversation and both Provincetown boats were telling it like they saw it.

The '*MARU*' was moving toward the '*Richard & Arnold*'. "Keep your fingers inside the rail," Dave yelled to Pete. "Either they have their radar on and are just being pushy or they don't see us and we're damn lucky." The big boat came within a foot of the railing as Dave and Peter stood watching. More heated words on the radio. Then Henry and Chris hauled in their gear and headed home.

"It was too bad they left, the next few tows were the biggest we'd seen in weeks. We unloaded the next morning a little over 8,000 pounds of white bellied beauties - flounder and yellow tail. The 'MARU' must have caught 40,000 lbs that night." Dave told me the following day.

The howling wind kept me awake all night as well, tossing and turning. "We were 'finest-kind'. No need to worry," Dave said to me as we sipped a cup of tea at the kitchen table. How could I not have dismal thoughts when I knew women who had lost husbands and sons on nights such as these? Would I ever learn to let go of the fear that sometimes creeps into my thoughts? I knew I had faith in my husband, but it was the greater faith that I needed to have more of. James Edmeston wrote in 1800 "Lead us, Heavenly Father, lead us. O're the world's tempestuous sea; Guard us, guide us, keep us, feed us, for we have no help but thee." I will say that prayer late at night when Dave has not yet come home from a fishing trip. It renews my faith, replacing my fears.

Then Dave said, "You can't run away from fish. When they're there, you stay. You only make money when the net is in the water and if the price of fish stays up because all the big boats are tied up because of a storm we might get paid over a dollar a pound for the fish, then we'll make a week's pay in one night. Makes up for the days when we can't get out. You know they call it fishing, rhymes with wishing not catching." I had to smile as we sat with cups of tea. I have had many sleepless nights listening to the wind. "You don't need to worry," he reassures me.

On nights in the late fall Dave and Peter could be found fishing to the east of the Highland when gale winds pushed them home. The two men stand inside the wheelhouse and talk about fishing inside the bay - closer to the lee shore. Dave would head the boat toward Truro. Sometimes the Coast Guard would show up, to check out what the boat is doing, to take a swift ride around the bay and to give us a head's up to watch the weather. Their boat comes along side, the cutter bouncing about like a cork in a bathtub. Then over the howling wind the radio crackles. "Winds Northeast, expected to increase to 60 knots," a voice is heard from the squawk box mounted over the windshield.

"I read you. Over." Dave holds the microphone then waves out the wheelhouse door. The guardsmen wave back, all is well. Dave and Peter watch the lights of the Coast Guard vessel as it heads back to Provincetown through the choppy seas and dark of night.

"Nice of them to check to see if we're ok," Dave grins at Peter. Inside the wheelhouse it is quiet and calm even though a howling gale is whipping up the dunes on the other side of the Truro hills. There is hardly a ripple on the water as the boat makes a circle and the net is set out again.

The next morning the two men unload five thousand pounds of flounder, it turned into a high powered night and one of good fishing. The boats from Provincetown are the first out after a storm has closed the fishing ground. Northeast storms can last a week, leaving huge swells that make it impossible to fish, unable to keep the net down because the boat is moving up fifteen foot seas. As the storm subsides and leaves the area it will give the smaller boats from Provincetown an opportunity to get to the fish first.

The small boat fleets around the northeast coast supported hundreds of families and took less fish than today's modern trawlers that support just a few. The commercial fishing industry has many differing views, many opinions as to how it should be run and many who think they know what is best for our oceans. Perhaps the issue is not who the fish belong to, but historically proven ways of maintaining balance in nature as well as in commerce. Then there are the environmental issues and those who would close our fishery altogether. There are the economic issues of jobs that must be considered. There are political and scientific views that must have a voice. And yet for over one-hundred years there has been abundance for the boats that fished from Provincetown. We need to take care of this precious resource and to do that we need to keep a working dialogue between all points of view. There will always be those who would take everything, using bigger and bigger, more and more efficient machines - the limits that have been placed upon fishermen are there for good reason, man is good at what he does. Yet for generations the Provincetown fleet, fished the Atlantic Ocean, Cape Cod Bay, the Middle Bank, the Stellwagen, and Nantucket Sound and never depleted the water of fish.

We live surrounded by grey liquid in winter, dark blue in spring, aqua in summer and green in the fall, where the sea gives up its bounty with little resistance to the men and women who go in search of flapping fish. The water that surrounds our peninsula is as much a part of our home, our lives and our spirits as is the boat, the town, and the house on the hill. There's an old saying among our fishermen, "When the fishermen make money there is prosperity everywhere."

The catch of the day can be anything. There are millions of varieties of sea life out there. Each as interesting as can be: little wiggly worms that move every part of their tiny bodies at once, fat sea creatures that look like vegetables, egg casings, vegetation of every description and fish so weird looking you'd think that you were on a different planet. Mollusks and man-eaters, if they're out there we catch them. Most of the exotic species get thrown right back and we watch them swim away. A rare Manta Ray came up in the net one summer day. It was more than 6 feet across, from black wing tip to black wing tip and had a notorious barbed tail that could inflict damage and pain if slapped against bare skin. We managed to get it back into the water within a few minutes by using an impromptu sling, a block and tackle that hoisted the two hundred pound beauty up and over the side. We watched this stranger, this summer tourist swim for safety toward the depths, wings gently pumping up and down.

Our nets are small and the amount of time in the water is short so it is possible for many species to survive a trip to the surface. The creatures that are not a part of the catch are thrown back into the sea. We've never caught a seal, a whale, a dolphin, a turtle, a sunfish, a great white, a sword fish or sea dragon, but because the Gulf Stream comes in close during summer months bringing varieties that do not make Cape Cod their year round home we have had visits from many unusual sea creatures.. One afternoon I spoke to Dave of the diversity of the oceans - in somber tones, telling him of my amazement and wonder at so many varieties and abundance. Dave replied, "Just like tourists in Provincetown on a hot summer day."

On one fishing trip we caught a flat faced blue-green fish called a dolphin, not to be confused with the mammal. I had never seen one before and had been told they were exceptionally good eating. It was saved for supper and when we returned to port in Martha's Vineyard that evening, a barbeque was prepared. The ten pound fish was gutted and wrapped with onions, tomatoes, and olives and put it on the grill. The aroma on the dock in Menemsha that night brought friends to the feast. It is true - most fishermen love to eat fish. It's a definite plus for remaining in the fish business. When Dave and I talk about getting out of fishing, I inevitably ask, "Where would I get my fresh fish?"

There is nothing as good as fresh fish to eat and Dave feels lucky to be able to do what he loves, but fishing has to be profitable. The boat has to catch enough fish to pay for fuel and maintenance and keep a crew working. If something goes wrong with the boat or engine it can mean weeks without a pay check. A big responsibility is keeping up with the care of the boat. The metal in the rigging, net reel and wenches corrodes fast in salt water. "Rust never sleeps," Dave is fond of saying. What is not seen on a wooden boat is the most important part of all. The bottom of the *'Richard & Arnold'* needs to be scrubbed and painted yearly. There are borer worms and barnacles that can damage the underside of a wooden boat and ducks will pull at the caulking to get at some tasty treat, all leading to leaks and water in the bilge.

The *'Richard & Arnold'* meant a decent life for us. When we first bought the boat a sweet Provincetown woman named Agnes Salvador told me, "You'll never get rich being a fisherman's wife, but you'll never want for anything." She said, "It takes a lot of faith, but if you have it, you'll always be happy." Agnes was the wife of Louie Salvador who fished most of his life with the 'Shirley & Roland'. They owned Louie's Seafood Float at MacMillan Wharf after retiring from fishing. Agnes was right. I've always been glad that we took the chance and cast our fate to the wind and waves. There have been times when it's been hard, times when money was tight, times when I worried for the safety of my husband and sons; but overall it's been worth it. Even the Federal government couldn't dampen my spirit because I have faith.

CHAPTER 5

Just When Things Were Looking So Good

Word spread from fisherman to fisherman around MacMillan Wharf to meet at the Community Center on Bradford Street at three o'clock on Friday afternoon. Two representatives from Washington, D. C. from the National Marine Fisheries Service would be there to explain to everyone what the government had in mind for us. David had been fishing the '*Richard & Arnold*' for three years and it was paying the mortgage for both the boat and for our home. Jackson was a budding teenager and Robert was already four years old. I was a busy working mother, but this meeting sounded like something I should attend, so I took the day off, left the boys with grandma and went to find out what was going on.

The fishing industry was at its zenith, the high point on the town wharf as fish trucks moved in and out of town daily. Vessels came and went from the harbor, both transient and town boats alike. There was talk in town of building a new wharf because boats were crowded, tying three and four deep along all the sides of the pier. Fishermen were not charged for using MacMillan Wharf because the town fathers felt that fishermen brought jobs and money to Provincetown. In exchange they were given a free berth. The men that attended the meeting were the backbone of the town, supporting the businesses, churches and schools.

In wool shirts, in an overheated room, on that blustery afternoon a hundred men sat on folding chairs waiting to hear what would be said. These were the guys who hauled in nets and wrestled scallop rakes, lifting hundred pound boxes of fish and ice on a daily basis. The men at the front of the room looked out at us, dressed and pressed in dark suits like they were going to the office or church, or a funeral.

One stepped up to a microphone, welcomed and thanked everyone for coming. "We are here from the United States Government and we're here to help you." His words sounded good. They began by telling us what tough shape the American fishery was in. They had the statistics, charts, graphs and they knew that many of us were having a difficult time bringing in the big catches as in past years. Everyone had to agree with what was being said. The fishermen knew the reality of fewer fish in the net. There was no mandate to take the pressure off the ground fish stocks, and yet many fishermen changed gear and targeted a different catch: scallops, clams or lobsters. Other fishermen just caught less and hoped the next tow would be better and some fishermen left the fisheries altogether for shore jobs. The fellows from NMFS struck at the heart of the matter and they had everyone's attention.

Provincetown's fleet consisted of mostly under powered, wooden boats that were built before World War II. Their size and hold capacity hadn't changed in fifty years. Some felt they didn't need tons of fish to make living, just good prices. The fellows from Washington explained that new rules and regulations governing the taking of this resource would be in place within the next six months.

"This resource belongs to all the people," they said. "The U.S. Government, with the passing of the Magnuson / Stevens Act in 1976, will control the taking of fish by foreign and domestic fleets within our 200 mile boundary." They smiled and we nodded our heads like children agreeing with every word. They encouraged us to look into underutilized species, the trash fish that is routinely thrown back such as: dogfish, ling- hake, eels, urchins and skates. The men in suits talked about changes in the mesh size for nets, record keeping, documenting tows and keeping track of how much fish is kept and what is shoveled overboard. "Everyone with a federal fishing permit will be issued a log book that must be filled out after each fishing trip and mailed back to our offices monthly. The data will be kept for statistical analysis." Then he said the words that got everyone's attention. "Look around the room men. In five years, half of you will be out of the fisheries. The government is looking for a 50% reduction in effort."

A stir went round the room, someone hollered out, "You can't do that". Others shook their heads in disbelief. Captain Rivers, owner of the 'Johnny O' stood up, and said, "We've been fishing around here longer than you've been alive and neither you nor any government agency is going to tell me what I can and can't do with my documented fishing boat."

Another fisherman stood and said, "This whole thing stinks. You're not pushing me out of the business." That pretty much ended the meeting.

Everyone got to their feet, some heading for the door, others milling around their seats, angry word could be heard above the din. David and I headed for the gentlemen in suits to meet the men who now controlled our future. Dave waited his turn and asked, "Is there any chance that things are not as bad as the picture you've painted here today?"

The man in the suit shrugged and said he hoped not, but it was important to downsize, to conserve, and to plan for sustainable yields. We were not sure what that meant, but the officials were polite, they'd already brought their message of doom and gloom to other ports and they knew the responses. They were polished and smiled at us as the systematic demise of the American Fishing Industry began.

Outside on the cemented front yard men huddled together, smoking cigarettes and talking in low voices. A mixture of Portuguese and English words could be heard, "I feel like something bad is happening. This is not right." The fishermen tried to understand all the D.C. guys had talked about. Restrictions and regulations! Some of these men couldn't keep accurate records for the boys in Washington, some couldn't write, some spoke broken English. "Why they want these records, anyway?" There were more questions than answers.

Most of the men in that room had fished their whole lives, learned from their fathers. One of the men said he knew what they could do with all those regulations. "I'm going to keep fishing like I have been doing all my life and if this resource belongs to all the people then let them invest $200,000 for a dragger and go out and chase fish like we do every day. These guys got it all wrong, there's plenty of fish." We had no moratoriums, no regulations, and no closures. The boats went out when they could and brought back as much as they could. Sixty boats called MacMillan Wharf home. The men fished long hours, took risks and made money for owners, crews and their families as well as many small businesses shore-side. It was one thing to talk about reducing the amount of fishing effort, but the reality was yet to hit home.

Before this meeting at the community center the fishery was open to anyone who wanted to invest in it, who had the interest and who thought they could make a living at it. The years leading to government intervention were fishing in its hay-day, like the last of the cowboys - the atmosphere was tinged with wildness. Then technology began blooming like algae on a hot day. The fishing boats got bigger. Americans had chased out the Russian factory trawlers and began replacing them with its' own. Then the real decline in stocks began. Some felt it was a cycle and that the ocean would repair itself if effort was made in other fishing areas such as scalloping or the underutilized species that the men in suits talked about. Some men knew they would leave fishing, sell out and move. Others saw a need for strict regulation. Like it or not changes were on the horizon. Suddenly our future became unclear and we began to wonder if we would still be fishing in five years.

On the way home from the community center Dave said, "I come from a long line of fishermen. My father died on his boat, my grandfather fished the Grand Banks in a dory. I can't imagine doing anything else." He took a deep breath and sighed, "What are we going to do?"

For me the answer was simple. "We are going to continue to be who we are. We are not going to give up. No matter what the D. C. guys tell us, we're doing ok. You're catching fish, making money and we're paying the bills. How bad can it be?" Doubts about being a fisherman were never part of the picture, but what I could not see was how it would affect us in the long run. I just couldn't believe that the government could force people out of the fishing business. There was no telling at the time how large the issue of fishing would become. For us, much of the talk inside the community center was just that, a lot of talk. Yet inwardly, we each hoped to be part of the fifty percent that would continue to fish.

In the days, weeks and months that followed the town fishermen questioned themselves, each other and the government. "If all the fishing boats were owner operated, maybe there would be no need for government intervention." "If they'd just let Mother Nature do her thing and leave us alone, things would even out." "Get rid of those factory trawlers and we'll all be better off." Dock talk and speculation about what was going to happen, left many scratching their heads and worrying about the future.

I felt that the feds got us mixed up with all those big off-shore fellows. "I have faith in our fellow man and the government. They know what they are doing, and some regulation will probably be a good thing. Fewer boats will mean better prices, right?" I said to Dave.

"This little fleet doesn't amount to a piss hole in a snow bank." Dave said. "The fish come and the fish go and have been for hundreds of years. We'll tighten our belts, fish less if need be, and cooperate by filling out all the paperwork." No one realized that a storm was brewing, that for years to come it would affect our lives and businesses, changing the face of our community. This was a tight-knit village that for generations had sent its men to fish the waters of Cape Cod Bay and the North Atlantic. Provincetown fishermen have always been respected in the community because they provide fish dollars to the town. Most of the money made from fishing stayed in town. Groceries, fuel, ice, clothes, knives, rope, baskets, buckets, wire, shackles, blocks, gloves and boots, bank notes, insurance, trucks for hauling and the thousands of small items that make a fishing business - supported our town. It has been estimated that for every dollar made in the fishing industry, seven dollars are generated within the town, from the deck of the boat to the table it is served on.

Each boat tied to MacMillan Wharf supported four to six families. Crewmen for each vessel kept the town supplied with fresh fish and prosperity. No one told these men when they could go out, how much they were allowed to catch, what type of gear to use, how many days they could fish and where they were allowed to go. Our fleet was regulated by Mother Nature. Sometimes you catch them and sometimes you don't, but you always try and we would keep trying.

Ups and downs have always been a part of the business and the new regulations, the log books and government over-seers would be just another part of the business. When fish were scarce, fishermen went for sea scallops or lobsters, they adapted. I didn't believe that fish were disappearing from the ocean, but I did understand that in order to maintain our supply of fish, steps would have to be taken to control the effort. Our fleet didn't chase fish to Georges Bank in the winter, we knew our limitations. The backbone of the town's economy was seafood; even the tourist industry depended on it. Our products were known to be the freshest, the firmest and tastiest: fish, scallops, clams, oysters, and our Cape Cod lobsters are the best. It is a tradition in Provincetown to give away as much fish as we can afford: to friends, family, neigh-bors, and strangers. It's considered good luck, but even that is changing.

We asked ourselves that day at the community cen-ter if these old boats could be responsible for the demise of the fishery. Some felt the rules and regulations were unjust and shouldn't pertain to us. None of what the feds had to say seemed real, like it was all happening to someone else, so mostly we went about our business of fishing and forgot about the predictions of doom and gloom espoused on that grey Friday afternoon at the community center.

CHAPTER 6

SHACK

Along with National Marine Fisheries Service, other government agencies began to focus on the coastal communities for different reasons. Most fishermen know that cash was paid under the table to most boats. A captain or owner would be happy to take part or all of his earnings in hard currency. Before statistics were kept on computers, before agencies with agendas put the fishery under a microscope, before fishing was labeled a bad thing, some fishermen chose to work out deals with their buyers to get paid partially or totally in cash. This 'SHACK' money came mostly from lobsters or scallops, the type of catch that did not go into the boxes to be shipped to New Bedford, Boston or New York.

Occasionally, the slip of paper that passed between buyer and seller would not show all the money that crossed their palms. Boxes of lobsters along with a few specialty fish like a large halibut or a handful of sea scallops made their way to the local seafood market where thousands of dollars were paid out in dollar bills stuffed into envelopes every Friday afternoon. And it was happening in every seaport community.

A few of the boat owners were taking cash money from the boxes of fish that were off loaded and shipped to cities as well. Money the crew didn't see would pass from hand to hand. Cash from the dealer could be as high as twenty cents a pound- under the table. This added up when the boats were unloading hundreds of thousands of pounds of fish. The amounts of cash varied of course, but it was not unheard of for 'SHACK' to run as much as $5000 to $10000 a week. A boat owner would sit down in the fish buyer's office, smoke a cigar, have a drink of whiskey and pick up his check, every Friday afternoon. No one knew what was in the envelope except those two men. Money in check or cash was given only to the owner who went home and figured out how much the crew had earned. Cash was frowned upon, but most crewmen turned a blind eye, glad to have their job. Some owners shared the cash from lobsters with crew, but some did not. An honest owner put the SHACK money into the stock to be given out in cash to crewmen on pay-day and most fishermen recorded it as part of the business.

'SHACK' was the word that brought the spotlight onto the fishing fleet like nothing else could have done. The dollars that no one was telling the IRS about came back to bite fishermen in the ass — big time. The IRS began looking closely at the fishing fleet records and it didn't take long before the unreported money was found. Some families had to sell their homes, boats and business to pay the tax and penalties. Dave tells me, "Figures don't lie, but liars figure."

Money was being made by boat owners, captains and crews, fish buyers, truckers, boatyards and the men who supplied oil, boxes, ice, gear, food, equipment, and everyone was spending fish dollars keeping the town economy humming. A dozen trucks carrying fish left the pier each night to make the morning markets in Boston and New York. Fish sales were in the hands of a few top players who set the prices according to supply and demand. It was always a guessing game as to how much money per pound the boat would be paid. Every Friday the boat received a check for what was unloaded during the previous week and no one except the fish buyer knew what the amount would be. Dave tells me that if the buyer's wife wanted a new car the price would drop dramatically. One year a fish-buyer told Dave that the price was low because everyone had left New York City that week, seems everyone had gone on vacation. The buyers set the price, but SHACK was negotiable.

The wharf was humming with business, boats and trucks, men and women coming and going and not many were keeping track of how much money changed hands, where the cash was going, who was getting what. There were fish-buyers handling thousands in cash each week. Their truck drivers carried guns to protect both the fish catch and the fish money. Boat owners were discouraged from using their own trucks to take fish to market, but a few men tried it anyway and found themselves hijacked at gun point, left on the side of the road, watching their catch disappear, lucky to be alive. The flow of cash from New York City was a win-win for those involved. Laundering money is not a new thing, the fish business was ripe for picking and cash was king. Everyone was getting their share, some reported, but most was not. The government began uncovering those who were spending more than they were making. I heard a story about a hearing in an IRS office in Boston, one fishermen was fined $60,000 and asked the agent if they would take a condo in Florida as payment. They did.

SHACK hurt fishermen in other ways as well. The federal government took a strong dislike to the way some fishing businesses were being conducted. Fishermen have a reputation as free thinkers, liking to do things their own way. These independent fishermen needed to be brought into line, observed and controlled and it was up to the government to see what was really going on in the fishing industry. When the government began to look more closely at how much fish was being caught and how much was actually reported, boat owners who did not report their catch, for whatever reason, lost licenses or were fined or both. It wasn't long before the National Marine Fisheries Service began using statistics and ratios - the amount of fish caught and reported, during a certain time frame, divided by some unknown factor- to cut up the fish pie. If you couldn't prove landings, because you were getting paid in cash, you didn't get a permit. No permit and you were out of the business! Done! More boats disappeared because licenses were removed.

It took a long time for 'SHACK' to disappear. The captains and crews loved to see those envelopes with a few hundred in cash. SHACK eventually came to an end, but the word was out - there was money to be made and this hurt the fishery in far reaching ways. Bigger and better boats began to appear, taking the place of the older less efficient machines. Using low interest government loans to capitalize on the fishing industry, men of wealth began investing in larger capacity, offshore vessels, changing the face of fishing. Until this time, most boats were owner-operator. Once it was discovered that a man in an office could make money by investing in a fishing boat, hiring a captain and crew, then lawyers, bankers, doctor and others began pouring money into the fish business, buying bigger boats and in return making money on their investment.

It didn't seem to matter that the men caught less fish because the prices got better. A Provincetown fisherman told me he was selling his boat and business because the days of the big catches were over. More Provincetown boats seem to fade away. Some left town on their own steam, sold and taken to distant harbors like the 'Gale' that went to South America. A few were left to Davy Jones, like the 'Porpoise' the 'Cape Star' that sunk in the harbor and the 'Pat Sea' and the 'Joan & Tom' sister ships that sank while tied to each other at the town wharf. Slowly the older boats began to disappear and more efficient, steel or fiberglass hulled boats came into the business. Then government intervention became a necessity. The huge wheels of government agencies and other non-government organizations began to grow in unimagined proportions. The bureaucracy grew as fish landings declined and more boats left the industry, melting into the shadows of history.

The '*Richard & Arnold*' has seen her share of 'SHACK'. It is hard to resist. There is nothing like bringing home an envelope filled with cash money to brighten the day as a justified reward for the hard work out upon the ocean. We took part of our money from lobsters in cash, sharing it with crew. Fortunately we reported all of our catch and paid our taxes. We gave up SHACK along with every other fisherman as regulations became stricter and the watchful eyes of government more stringent. Like all good citizens of this great country Dave and I learned to live with the rules.

"When the government throws out another regulation, we'll adjust the set of our sails," Dave said as I placed the daily mail from the National Marine Fisheries onto the kitchen table. As bureaucracy grew from hundreds of government employees to thousands, the controls got tighter, strangling the independent fisherman so that more boats left the industry, vanishing along with 'Shack'. While Dave and I went about our lives, we were unaware that the downsizing of our fishery, the sunset and nautical twilight - had begun.

CHAPTER 7

Glorious Squid

Every spring the squid return to Nantucket Sound. Every year, like clockwork, they make their way up the coast. Even before man was marking down on paper the habits of sea creatures, our shores were the place for squid to come to eat or be eaten, to be caught, to spawn and to die. And every year, like clockwork, the same guys show up with the same boats to chase the illusive squid. As new boat owner with a note to pay, Dave did what was needed to keep the business profitable. He went squid fishing for the first time in 1982 just after we bought the 'Richard & Arnold'. Never did he imagine that he'd see so many boats in one place doing the same thing.

There were hundreds of fishing boats in every size, from a twenty foot skiff towing wire baskets, to one hundred-twenty foot factory trawlers. Boats from Massachusetts, Rhode Island, Connecticut and New York, New Jersey and as far away as North Carolina were there to fill their hulls with squid. Everyone had a shot at making money. Year after year we all hope for a good squid season to bail us out from the winter money woes. The catch can vary from almost nothing to thousands of pounds. It's a game of roulette, a toss of the dice or another tow; you just never know what will be in the net. The same hard-working, hard-core, hard-living men that share the small harbors of Hyannis, Falmouth and Martha's Vineyard have grown to know one another with the passing of seasons. Some of the squid fishermen have their own rituals and some invent new ones as they go.

Dave and I have a tradition each spring. He will point to the oak trees in the yard and tell me, "When the buds on the oak are as big as a mouse's ear, the squid are near."

Then I do the 'squid dance'. I shake and move my body in what I think resembles a squid, to a happy beat and sing, "Squid, squid, squid!" Then our hopes for a profitable season are off to a good start. Squid fishing is not like other types of fishing that Dave is involve in, it is unique in many ways. Dave might catch up to ten-thousand pounds for a day and have to stop midday because that's all one man can handle or he may have no squid at all. We hire crewmen when we can find them, but it's a hit or miss business. It's difficult to keep good crew when they might not make money for weeks at a time. Squid season can mean not needing any help or wishing there were two other guys on deck. The *Richard & Arnold*' has had lots of great crew members over the years and both our sons have helped shovel squid.

Dave loves squid season because it reminds him of what Provincetown was like when he was growing up. Fisher-folk spent all their free time at the wharf or on their boats. They work on nets, tell stories, give advice and help one another. At the Woods Hole dock, squid season brings men together from all over the east coast to joke, tell tales and bond in the particular way that fishermen do. Many of the captains and crews live on board, continuing the comradeship when not fishing.

Dave stays on the boat twenty-four-seven, coming home when he's had enough, usually every four or five days. It's like camping. Dave's hands get stained with ink; his clothes smell of the sea, of salt and of squid. After working a week picking up squid his clothing is stiff enough to stand up on their own and I have to throw them away because I can never get the smell or the ink out. He's tired all the time, but he will talk with the other fishermen for hours. He'll complain about everything, but loves every minute of it. The season is short - a month or two - then the boats return to their home ports.

Squid fishing begins early when you live on board. At 3 a.m. Dave gets tea and does the morning ablution, washing up using a basin and water heated on the stove. Next he will check the boat's oil and water, bilge and battery, then start up the engine and let it warm while he does a deck check. Stepping into the tiny wheelhouse he turns on the electronics; radar, autopilot and now we have a computer with tracking device. When all is ready he lets go the lines and heads out into Woods Hole Channel. The '*Richard & Arnold*' turns east toward the glow of light as twilight begins.

Every squid season is the same, yet they are all different. It could be a great year with good prices, or it could be a broker. Squid are eaten around the world by people and sea creatures. They are pure protein and delicious. We are paid a varying price which can be as high as $2.00 a pound to the boat or as low as 20 cents a pound. Two weeks into the squid season the price begins to drop, and then drops again and then again until they are not worth going out for. As squid season was about to get underway, Dave and I were having tea and reminiscing. I reminded Dave of the year we didn't make a profit because the price dropped to twenty cents. "At least we didn't go backward and I got to make a great squid stew for supper," I said.

Dave replied, "You mean I got to work my ass off for nothing but the fun of it and get bamboozled by fish buyers on top of that?"

I gave him a pat on the back and said, "The boat always gets its share, so you got the new radar that year and I got to make fried squid rings and squid stew. It balances out in the end." I have learned that fishing can be an 'all or nothing' undertaking and it is always better to keep an optimistic outlook and a cushion of money in the bank. Squid are not limitless and when the run is gone, it's gone. Some years there is great abundance and other times you can't find a squid for trying. The amount of natural predation goes beyond anything the fishing fleet can catch. Everything with a fin or gill eats squid. These creatures are on the low end of the food chain and are eaten by everything larger. They feed the underwater world as well as man in his mansions.

Preparations for the season begin in March, but the squid usually don't show up until April or May, depending on the temperature of the water, the flow of the currents, the amount of sunlight and Mother Nature. Checking hydraulic hoses, replacing shackles that are rusting, examining lines that might have frayed during the winter storms are a part of the preparation for the madness called squid. Nets will be changed. If we didn't haul the boat in the fall or winter it will need to go onto a cradle at the boat yard. The bottom needs to be kept in sound condition. Scraping, caulking or packing 'oakum' into the seams, then tarring and painting to keep the boat watertight is the headache of a wooden boat owner. It is a big expense but a necessity. The haul out can cost the last of our savings, so we hope for a good fishing year, we keep the faith. It doesn't matter what the spring weather or how much money we have left in the bank or what is happening in the rest of the world, we get ready for another squid season and I do my spring squid dance while David gets the boat ready.

When the 'Richard & Arnold arrives at Woods hole dock Dave will call or radio one of the other boats asking if anyone has been out fishing, testing the water. The men call each other regularly on their CB radios and now on cell phones. All conversation between the fishermen is of fish, boats and squid. One year every sentence across the airwaves ended or began with the word squid. "How'd that tow look, Squid," called Hokey on his CB. "Good, go ahead, squid," answered Mike from his white and red wheelhouse, then came, "Squid dance tonight in the parking lot, squid." The radio crackled with laughter. A number of boats got into the act. "They're catching squid from skiffs under the lights. Squid!" Following more laughter, "Anyone hear the price, yet? Squid!" Then one of the guys will put one of those laughing boxes next to the mike for thirty seconds while everyone listens to the absurd noise. Sometimes the chatter goes on for hours and sometimes there are hours of radio silence.

Early spring weather brings weeks of fog and cold, damp days. Fishing and waiting for the first hit of squid can get boring, but the boats keep moving up and down in the same area, hour after hour, marking time, anticipating the first strike. Some men talk on the radio, others make minor repairs and some listen to their own thoughts and daydream for hours. Many of the smaller boats have just the captain on board until the squid show and then crews will be found.

Nets are designed, built, swapped, bought and sold. One year a man approached Dave after he was tied up at the Woods Hole dock. The stranger said that he just bought the abandoned boat tied in front of the 'Richard & Arnold'. "I'm not planning on going fishing and there is a net on the deck that I don't know what to do with." He offered the net free of charge, "Just get it off the boat and it's yours." David debated taking the net when he saw it piled on the stern of the derelict fishing boat. It looked bigger than any of Dave's regular nets and he would have to wrestle it into the lazarette in the stern, but because David is very practical, he knows that it is a good thing to have a spare net. He took the fellow up on the offer and brought the 'Richard & Arnold' alongside the derelict boat and hoisted the net across the rails, using the boat's boom and tackle lines, from one boat to the other, in small increments, and then he replaced his usual net with the free-be, just to see how it would work.

Dave used the net the next day and called me late that evening after he had unloaded his catch to tell me about it. He could hardly stop laughing. He said, "You should see this net. I caught more fish in one tow with that net than I had all the previous day. I wish you'd been here." His voice was full of excitement, "I think this net was an experiment, made by the scientists at Woods Hole Oceanic Institute or someone with quite an imagination. It took me awhile to figure it out. It has two bags attached to the body. I've never seen anything like it." I waited for him to stop laughing, "It looked like two big tits hanging in the air filled to the brim with squid."

But the next night when he called he didn't sound as enthusiastic, "It's just like every other net, filled every mesh with seaweed, it was more to handle and heavy as hell." He had to wrestle twice the twine without twice the help for half the amount caught. He told me that when the net plugs up with seaweed it gets heavy and collapses on itself - closing the mouth and this two-tit net did just that.

I arrived in Woods Hole Harbor a few nights later to bring Dave home for R&R. We took the strange net home with us. He's tried using the experimental net a few times since then, but the same thing happens, it clogs up. Dave has to pick out the seaweed from every mesh so that it will be light enough to keep from collapsing. More work than it is worth and too heavy for one guy to handle. For a long time the strange net sat in a pile in the yard. Then one day Dave began using it for parts and built another squid net, more to his liking.

Squid tows are different because the boat pulls the net in the same direction as the tide. The boat then turns, hauls in the net and steams up against the current to some unknown spot to begin again. The captains all know each other and hail each other as they pass starboard to starboard, or port to port. Sometimes the boats come close enough for men to yell at each other as they go by. They might wave their arms a number of times to count off the number of bushels or baskets in that tow - measuring their catch against each other. When boats are working in a small area of water it can get crowded. I'm amazed there aren't more accidents, especially when every-one is on deck shoveling squid or working at lowering boxes into the fish-hold. One year the 'Carol A' was towing one way, and the 'Scuttlebutt' was steaming up-tide when - bang, they bounced off each other. Not much damage, no one hurt, they were lucky. It was just a ricochet, red paint on the blue boat like a fender-bender in the traffic world. A continuous lookout should be kept when there is not much room to ma-neuver, but many boats have only one man onboard. On the *'Richard & Arnold'* Dave sets the auto pilot, bends over the pile of squid and keeps a lookout by simply raising his head and look-ing to see where everyone else is.

Squid are the joy and the agony of spring. They can lift your heart and give you the impetus to keep fishing or they can leave you broke and depressed. There is small ring of time that will contain squid and you hope your boat is in the right place at the right time. Squid provide us with food and they give us the cash to pay the mortgage. Many seasons Dave will unload 3,000 pounds of squid every day, all by himself. After four nights sleeping aboard, I drive round-trip one-hundred and fifty miles to pick him up and bring him home for a good food, a hot shower and a night in his own bed. The next morning I drive him back to the boat so he won't miss a day.

On one ride home he told me how tired he was. "I'm not getting enough sleep because every night families show up with generators, lights and skiffs. I don't mind that, but they walk across my boat and holler at each other while they are fishing. I went on deck the other night and scared the hell out of one old man. I had to holler to get him off my boat. I don't think he liked that, but God I'm tired." I could see the lines of his face and the slump of his shoulders.

"Maybe they don't know that all the boats have guys sleeping on them," I tried to sound sympathetic. "Or worse, maybe they don't care. They could be squid starved!" I don't think Dave enjoyed the humor.

On the way back to the boat the next day, we stopped at Sears and bought a generator. "I'll let it run all night to drown out the voices, it's worth a try." It did the trick. He now sleeps well with the white noise in the background and other people get to fish for squid off the dock.

Dave was having one of those seasons trying not to get discouraged. He began driving his truck so that I didn't have to spend all my time traveling back and forth across the cape. He'd called and said, "I'm coming home to pick up a different net from our yard." He drove for ninety minutes, loaded a different net into his pickup truck, and then drove back to unload it onto the boat. He fished all day but still caught no squid. So the next day he drove back home again. This trip was to pick up and change the doors, the large metal slabs that hold the net open. He played with the net and doors for days, adding more floats to the head rope, adjusting the wire - and in the end it paid off. When he finally started catching squid and was back in the running, catching a thousand pounds in one tow, the State of Massachusetts closed the area. That squid season was over for us. As much as we hated it, we would have to wait until the next year for squid.

The camaraderie at the dock can be a fun time. The men get together to share meals and stories. They talk fish and boats as fishermen have for generations, helping each other with equipment, engine parts and giving plenty of advice. Some of the guys are practical jokers as well. One night Mike and Bobby nailed the tie up lines of the boat 'Ripper' to the poles at the wharf in Woods Hole. They used six-inch spikes to be sure they wouldn't get pulled out by the big Caterpillar engine as the boat backed away from the berth. Early the next morning the captain came out on deck and hollered at his crew, "Let the lines go!" He went back into the wheelhouse to maneuver the boat away from the dock. "What the hell is taking you so long?" Jack's son was pulling at the lines, trying unsuccessfully to remove them. Captain Jack hollered again to get the lines off the pole. He watched his son struggling with the rope, then not able to contain his impatience, Captain

Jack grabbed at the line and pulled. He knew at once what was happening! The captain furrowed his bushy black eyebrows and looked out over the wharf to see who was laughing at him! Everyone was! It was a struggle but the lines came off the poles and eventually the 'Ripper' with captain and crew spent the day catching their share of squid.

The fun was done in good spirit with never a bad intention, but one day a prank almost caused a real problem. Late one afternoon two boats were heading to the Sandwich Basin inside the Cape Cod Canal, home from a squid trip. The Canal is a narrow waterway cut into the land, making Cape Cod an island. The *'Sol-E-Mar'* and the *'Millpoint'* were side by side and they both knew that whoever got to the dock first - would unload first. The race was on! The captains, Mike and Hokey, pushed the throttle as far as they dared. Somewhere in the middle of the canal a cherry bomb exploded in midair. The sound echoed against the rocks like an explosion. Not to be outdone, the captain of the second boat reached into the drawer under the dash and pulled out a small fire-cracker. A volley began, each boat popping off a couple of Fourth of July fireworks. Like pirates and buccaneers they were enjoying the spirit of the race.

Then a cherry-bomb landed on the deck of the 'Millpoint' at the bow and rolled down the side and out the scupper. There was a large BOOM as it hit the water. Captain Mike stepped out of the wheelhouse, leaning over the rail, he looked at the side of his boat. He was shocked by what he saw. A plank was sticking out from the side of his pocket dragger, right at the waterline. The blast's shock wave had caused the wood to pop away from the side of the hull. Mike radioed to his racing buddy to stand-by while he checked the bilge. He didn't like what he saw, water pouring in over the floorboards.

If this had happened at sea the boat might have sunk, but the saving grace was the short distance to the Sandwich Basin, a few minutes to where the Coast Guard was standing-by with a pump. The Harbormaster helped arranged for a haul-out and repairs were made in short time. In the end, it turned out to be a good thing because the next winter Mike had the entire boat covered with fiberglass. The captain would sleep well, never again worrying about popping a plank, with or without a cherry bomb. Years later we laughed when he told me, "I don't hold a grudge because I got to unload first!"

The imagination of squid fishermen is topped only by their sense of humor. Dave came home one year from a squid trip to teach me and the boys how to build a 'spudzuka'. The boys were all eyes and ears as Dave explained, "The fellows are always looking for new forms of entertainment as they go back and forth in the same area hour after hour. One of the guys came up with this gadget." He started laughing. "You take this plastic pipe and stuff a potato in one end......." I didn't stay to hear anymore, but after a couple of minutes I heard a boom and from my kitchen window saw a potato fly fifty yards across the tree tops into the neighboring field. Dave was telling our sons how the guys were shooting them at each other across the tops of the waves as the boats passed each other. When men go fishing for squid they are a different breed. They are either so busy they don't have time to eat or it is just the opposite and they sit in the wheelhouse watching the water pass under the hull dreaming up ways to keep each other laughing.

During a rather slow squid season, Jack of the *'Ripper'* decided it was a good day to run the stars and stripes up the main mast. His American flag stood out against the blue sky as the boats passed each other in their hourly parade. When Mike on board his boat saw the flag he went below and retrieved his American flag as well as the flag of Great Britain, attaching them to a running line that went to the top of the mast of the *'Millpoint'*. The fellows were getting into the swing of things. Next in the parade of boats came Danny with a Portuguese flag under the American flag on the mast of the *'Karen Ann'*.

Dave aboard our *'Richard & Arnold'* dug out his favorite flags: an American flag, a Portuguese Flag and another that he hangs up for the Provincetown Festival the last weekend in June. Our mermaid flag, a creation of our friend the Creative Seamstress of Truro, has a woman sewn onto old sailcloth, with long hair, fish-fin legs and two naked breasts. She is a treat to the mariners' eyes. Every boat could see her flapping in the breeze. The fleet was getting into the spirit of the day, but the best was yet to come.

When Carol and David on board their boat, *'Francis Elizabeth'* motored past, in its rigging flew a union suit, the long johns worn to keep you warm in winter. The captain was standing on deck in his underwear and black boots. He had a small American flag on a stick and gave each passing vessel a salute as they towed in the opposite direction. David and Carol won the best decorated boat award that year.

This year Dave will prepare as usual, we will dig out the right nets, check over the rigging and do the squid-dance. We are hoping the squid will come early and stay late. Many of the men that fished for squid alongside the '*Richard & Arnold*' will not be returning this year. They will be sorely missed. David and Carol have moved to greener pastures. Joe, Bobby and 'Millpoint' Mike have retired their boots. Whiskey Man, Jean, Louie, and Ray have tied their lines to the wharf for the last time.

We've said good-bye to our friends Hokey and his son Billy, Captain Speedy, Captain Randy, Rock Tom and Danny. They have crossed the bar — "twilight and evening bell and after that the dark, and may there be no sadness of farewell, when I embark," as Lord Alfred Tennyson wrote in 1890. I am afraid this squid season will be a little lonely, a little quiet and not nearly as much fun.

*Wildflower Blessing
of the Fleet 1972*

Wildflower with Captain Dave
Fishing 1976

Richard & Arnold Fishermen's Wharf,
Provincetown 1982

Richard & Arnold Blessing
of the Fleet 1983

Richard & Arnold Provincetown
Harbor 2009

Richard & Arnold, 1937

CHAPTER 8

Fishing with Family

Whether it is squid, flat fish, scallops or lobster our family fishing tradition began long ago with David's father and grandfather. Dave began fishing when he was just a boy looking for adventure and so it was a natural progression that both of our sons would fish aboard the *'Richard & Arnold'*. Jackson has known what life aboard a boat is like since he was a toddler and when our second son Robert was just six months old, the family took a vacation trip onboard the boat.

It was a warm July day when we went to see the Tall Ships at Newport, Rhode Island. Jackson was an experienced twelve year-old mariner. He brought his friend Jesse and the five of us lived on the *'Richard & Arnold'* for one week. The quarters below deck are small but warm and comfortable. A curtain is used to divide the bunks for privacy. "Just like camping," Dave told the boys, "Only on water." Dave, the baby, and I slept and changed in the bow on our double bunk. The older boys each had a bunk along the port side, one up, one down. There is a private head, the toilet for landlubbers, and the galley has a sink, a stove, a cooler and a table with built in benches — all to keep the crew happy and well fed. A forward hatch catches the breeze, cooling us in the July heat. We had our sleeping bags, plenty of food and a supply of pampers. What more could you ask for?

This turned out to be a busmen's holiday. Coming through the Cape Cod Canal and heading into Buzzards Bay I was looking out the windows of the wheelhouse, holding the little one when Dave suggested we make a tow outside Martha's Vineyard and then head to Menemsha for the night. "We might even make enough to pay for the trip and Jesse will get to see what fishing is all about." Dave said. There was no set schedule. We had a week of vacation and this would put our arrival in Newport at mid-day instead of after dark. It made sense. Dave brought the '*Richard & Arnold*' close to the island and set the net in the area around Gay Head where he had fished many times before. For two hours the boat dragged the net around as we watched the colorful layers of cliffs at the tip of the island pass by. When the net was finally brought over the rail and the fish dumped onto the deck the older boys helped, getting completely soaked while picking up fish.

Jesse exclaimed, "WOW. What's this?"

Dave was patient, "That's a scup, too small, throw it back." After more exclamations and questions Dave gave the boys a lesson in fishing. "That's a sea robin, watch out for those barbs on its head. We don't keep those, throw it back. That's a fluke but it's too small, throw it back too." The captain showed the crew how to measure the fish using a wooden board shaped like a paddle that had a mark at 14 inches. "Anything smaller than that gets thrown back," he told them.

In their shorts and boots they were up to their knees in mud, shells, and fish. They pushed and pulled the heavy baskets forward to be washed with the deck hose. The fish were then dumped into a container of salt water and ice to keep them fresh. While Dave headed the boat toward the harbor, the boys squirted each other with the deck hose to rinse off the mud and fish smells that accumulated while picking through the pile. Their youthful faces radiated fun, surprise and life, giving Dave and me the best reason for having a fishing boat

It was midafternoon when we tied the lines around the poles inside Menemsha Harbor on Martha's Vineyard. I took the three boys to the beach for a swim and then for hot showers at the town maintained bathrooms. Dave took care of the fish and the boat, and then headed to Squid Row where some of the best fishermen on the east coast swap stories and fish tales. Our vacation was off to a good start.

When we returned from cleaning up, the 'Quicksa Strida' was taking out Swordfish. We watched in awe as the big fish were lifted into the back of a waiting truck. Jonathan and his brother Greg land more swordfish than anyone else and are considered high-liners on the island. They have what it takes: knowledge, experience, as well as a certain knack for catching the giants. My young fishermen got up close and touched the big sea creatures. Each fish weighed in at over four hundred pounds and there were dozens of them. I heard Jackson tell his friend Jesse that he would sure like to catch a fish like that someday.

When the big fish had all been unloaded, we returned to our boat, stepping over the rail onto the deck of the '*Richard & Arnold*'. In our homeport of Provincetown the average tide runs ten feet, so we are used to climbing ladders to get on and off the boat. The docks in Menemsha are a delight for us. With just three and four feet of tide, land is just a couple of steps away. I marvel at the difference in tides in different areas around the world, some as big as forty feet in the Bay of Fundy in Nova Scotia, Canada where I saw a freighter sitting on the sand waiting for the tide to come in and some like the Menemsha docks where we step easily off the boat. Of course David is there to lend a helping hand for a wife with a six month old son, no matter how high the tide.

Dave took our fish to Larson's Fish Market, where for generations fishermen are welcomed by a pretty young woman in dungarees and knee-high black boots, named Betsy. She's ready with a smile and a helping hand. It is always a pleasure to tie in Menemsha where the atmosphere is clean, salty and friendly.

The next morning after breakfast we left the tiny harbor for the trip across the sound. It was so rough that Jackson, Jesse and I were seasick. The baby sat on the chart table next to Dave in the wheelhouse, making sounds and laughing. We had rigged a net to make a sort of playpen where baby Robert sat happily watching daddy and the waves. Eventually the seas calmed and so did our stomachs and we turned westward toward Newport Harbor. The sight that greeted us took all thought of sickness away.

We entered the harbor with a line of boats looking for a berth, hoping to see the magnificent vessels brought here from all over the world. The harbor was filled to capacity with every kind of floating device known to man. Hundreds, maybe thousands, of boats were gliding or tied inside the harbor. The air held excitement, sun and color. Dave spotted what appeared to be a commercial pier to our starboard and the only empty place in view. He maneuvered the boat alongside the wooden pier and we began tying ropes to the poles. We were placing the stern line on a wharf pole when a gentleman with white hair leaned over the edge and said, "I'm sorry this is a private dock." I stepped from the wheelhouse with Robert in my arms. The man said, "You can't tie here." I nodded that I understood and looked toward Dave.

Dave said, "Sorry about that." He and the two boys went to undo the lines. The gentleman on the pier stood over us, watching, as Dave told the youngsters what to do.

Then the man on the wharf asked, "Is this the '*Richard & Arnold*' out of Provincetown?" When Dave said yes, the man gave us a big smile, "I used to fish alongside this boat when it was owned by Frank Parson." We listened as he continued, "She has hardly changed, looks good. Are you still fishing with her?"

When Dave said he was fishing every chance he got, the older man said, "You all stay as long as you want." He told us he had fished on the Grand Banks and on the Middle Bank.

"It's good to see the boat is being taken care of. You and your family have a good time while you're here in Newport." He tipped his cap to us and was gone before we could thank him and we never got his name.

Captain Dave turned to the boys, "Let's get the skiff in the water. We'll use the winch to lift it. You boys hold the guide line. It's a team effort." The skiff was lifted over the side and within minutes was bobbing next to the *Richard & Arnold*. "Well done boys. We looked like professionals." The young men grinned from ear to ear.

I turned to face the harbor, taking it all in for the first time. I was standing close to some of the most magnificent vessels in the world. I could almost reach out and touch them. Flags and pennants of brightly colored cloth flapped in the breeze from the mastheads. Here we were - berthed twenty feet from one of the main attractions. It was awesome and inspiring. Thank goodness the *Richard & Arnold* had been cleaned and painted before we left Provincetown. I knew in my heart that we were representing our community and I felt so proud of my home, my boat and my fishermen.

It was the world's fair of sailing. Training ships from countries around the world filled the space of Newport Harbor. They were regal, magnificent and majestic. There was motion everywhere, movement of boats, people, and flags. I felt that we were at the center of the maritime world. One of our boys asked, "Where are they from?"

Dave pointed at boats, calling out names and places. "On the mooring, off the port bow is the *'Eagle'* representing the United States. There's the *'Esmeralda'* from Chile, and the one tied in front of us is the *'Amerigo Vespucci'* from Italy. We spotted flags from Canada, Great Britain and a few we didn't recognize. They were displayed at the sterns or topmasts of schooners and windjammers. Dave went into the foc'sle and brought a triangular wrapped cloth of stars and stripes out with him. "Who's for raising the flag?" We all gave a rousing holler and Dave ran up our colors on the tackle line to the top of the mast. "Let's get a closer look," the captain said. We put on our life jackets. I held an umbrella to keep the sun from our little Robert. Dave rowed from the center seat, Jackson and Jessie sat in the stern and the baby rested in a sling in my arms as we perched comfortably in the bow of our skiff. We joined the sightseers and the sights.

Jackson and Jessie were making sounds that were joyful to my ears. "Wow, look at the carvings! Wow, can we get closer?" Looking up at the sides, bows and sterns of these seagoing vessels was like seeing history carved in the wood. One ship had small leaded windows in the lazarette, the small area in the stern that in large vessels is often used as Captain's quarters. A small doorway led to where only the imagination could take us. We were all eyes and ears that afternoon as we looked at life upon the waters from another perspective. These ships carried thousands of square feet of sail, were crewed by hundreds of adventurous men representing their counties. I felt the pride on our National Heritage and felt for the first time the brotherhood of seamen.

The next morning the *'Amerigo Vespucci'* prepared to leave. The five of us sat on the rail watching and listening as hundreds of midshipmen climbed the masts to stand shoulder to shoulder in the rigging of this great Barque. They waited silently. And then, at the sound of a pipe whistle, they began to sing. We could hear the voices harmonizing in the Sunday morning hush that engulfed the harbor. The sound of many young people as one voice filled the air. The three-mast, square rigged ship slowly began moving away from the dock. As the harbor grew still, the voices grew louder. I listened first to sea-shanties and then as their magnificent vessel began to depart the harbor, their National Anthem "Fratelli d'Italia". I felt my throat catch, tasting tears, as a sail was unfurled the voices began to fade. The ship move away and was gone. We stayed for two days, enjoying this beautiful town, and then with hearts filled to the brim, we set our course for Provincetown and home.

We continued along our usual course after returning to our homeport- fishing, working, raising two boys - so that the days flowed into weeks, then months and years. Then one day my husband came into the kitchen and asked me what I thought of having our son Jackson crew aboard the *'Richard & Arnold.'* Dave said, "Weekends and school vacations." He had obviously been thinking this over. "He's old enough and would be a big help." The thought made me nervous, then queasy. I paced back and forth through the house without answering. Our son was becoming a man. He was in high school and changing in body and mind. "We need to keep him out of trouble and help him know his own strengths." Dave sounded like he'd already made up his mind.

I answered, "I think you should ask Jackson. If he wants to go, I don't think it would be right to hold him back." Of course Jackson's answer was yes, the young man wanted a job to make the money that would buy him the 'Pontiac Trans-Am' he was dreaming about. Both of our boys have spent time aboard the boats from very young ages, but until this time they had never fished as crew, unsupervised by mom. We both knew he was capable. The family had been together many times for summertime fishing, easy fishing with warmer water and calmer seas, but Dave was talking about something else.

Jackson was fourteen when he made his first fishing trip that came with pay. Our second son, Robert was in Kindergarten and I was working at the school. Jackson was given a half crew-share because we didn't want him to hurt himself with too much spending money. We helped him start a bank account, encouraging him to save. There were times when Jackson didn't want to go fishing, when it was rough, wet or cold, or when he'd rather be hanging out at the beach with his friends, but he never complained. His experiences taught him how to handle the boat and he was proud of his work at the end of the week when he was handed a check. Jackson fished when he could throughout his high school years, even when Dave had other crewmen. I struggled with the idea of him out there on an old boat and my imagination sometimes ran rampant, so I said little prayers throughout the day.

One evening Dave's pickup truck pulled into the yard. He and Jackson had been fishing since dawn and I knew they'd be hungry and tired. Jackson is a strong crewman and excited about everything, jumping in to help even when not asked. It was just about suppertime when Jackson bounced into the house and told me to come see what they had for me. My fishermen had big smiles and big greetings, "You should see what we brought home. They're in the back of the truck," my son said. I am thinking of a bucket of sea clams or a lobster that won't fit into the cook pot. "Come see," he added.

Robert was out the door in bare feet jumping into his father's arms as I stepped from the kitchen door. Dave swung our young son into the back of the truck and looked at me, "Where do you want them?" I am speechless once again. There are four huge boulders sitting in the back of the pickup. Together they weighed enough to test the springs of the ¾ ton truck and they were beautiful. "I thought you might like them for your garden," Dave smiled. Robert began climbing on the rocks, while I tried to find words.

"Something to hold down the dirt in a Northeaster?" I asked. "How thoughtful of you!" I was thinking that these boulders would make seats, a wall or decoration. "I'll think where to put them while you tell me how you came by these massive pieces of stone. Let's hear the story while I get supper together." I gave them each a hug and we walked to the kitchen.

They both started talking at once. Dave smiled and let his number one crewman tell the story. "They came up in the net. Dad slung them with ropes to get them inside the boat. I helped." Jackson told me. "They must weigh five hundred pounds apiece." I am amazed that these rocks came up in the net without ripping and falling through. Dave reminds me that objects have buoyancy.

"When there is a big rock in the net, it jolts and bounces causing a change in the forward momentum, I could sense something wasn't right." The captain added, "I figured once they were inside the boat, no sense putting them back to catch again. When they reach the deck they're half way home anyway." Dave stopped to give me a kiss, "Besides if I cut the net open to let them fall back into the water I'd have lost the few fish that were in the net, and you know how I hate to let fish go once I've caught them."

After supper we walked around the yard and then I pointed to where I thought the stones should go. Dave tied a rope around them, then tied the rope to the fence and drove the truck away. It was quick. One by one they pounded onto the ground, permanent additions. The boys and I watched the four gifts from the sea tumble to a place near the grape vines. "Don't worry," Dave said. "If you don't like them, I can always take them back to where they came from."

"I would never part with one of them," I said. "But did you bring any fish?" That night around the kitchen table after giving thanks for the bounty of the oceans, the safety of our family and for the beautiful additions to my garden, we ate the catch of the day. The stones were set in their honored place, the supper dishes were done, the boys were getting ready for bed when I remembered, "Oh, by the way, we got another letter from the National Marine Fisheries Service today, it addresses us as: Dear Maritime Partner. It has something to do with 'rolling closures'. You'd better read it. I can't figure it out."

"Partner?" Dave questioned, "I don't see them out on my deck, do you? I wonder how they justify that. The only partners I'll ever have are our sons, Jackson and Robert." We laughed, but I knew this was serious, "Seems like there is something new every day now, it's getting hard to keep up with the regulations." We were receiving letters from NMFS daily.

This piece of mail told us that some of the areas we fish in would be closed for three months of the year. "Looks like I'm not going to be allowed to fish September, October and November." Dave shook his head, "How can this be? That's our best time for fishing." Even though we agreed that regulations are needed to provide a sustainable fishery for future generations, we had a bad feeling about what was happening to our community fishery. "Our profits will be much less this year. I'm going to have to come up with a way to make up the loss." I was frightened by what I was unable to understand. The letter showed charts of the areas we regularly fished, some shaded with dots, some with stripes and others shaded with shadow, each with dates of closures.

"Thank you for the stones," I said to my family of fishermen. Then Jackson told us that he'd saved enough to buy the Pontiac Firebird he had his eye on. We couldn't say no, he'd earned every penny. Jackson was growing, old enough to drive, becoming a fine young man, independent like his dad. When he learned that we had to telephone the government when we wanted to go out fishing he said, "Too much government in the business can't be a good thing." It was 1989; he was graduating high school in May, and would soon be leaving home to enter the University of Maine where he would set his sails for other horizons, but not until after taking a few more fishing trips with his father.

Our sons would always be Dave's fishing partners, helping when they could. Robert fished with his father in much the same way that his older brother did, only ten years later. At fourteen years of age Robert had his own boat, a sixteen foot open skiff with a fifteen horsepower Evinrude engine. He had a student permit for lobster trapping and he knew how to hook a fish. One autumn afternoon he asked Dave if it would be ok for him to go jigging for mackerel up in the cove. The plan was to take along his friend Arthur, anchor up and the two young men would jig with a hook and line. Dave said in a joking way, "If you load up with fish, I'll have to get you a bigger boat." I watched the two young men and boat get smaller as they headed away from the pier. Dave turned to me and said, "Remember the time he fished for flounder off the stern of the '*Richard & Arnold*' while we were at anchor? He asked us how many fish we wanted for supper."

"Yes. He tried for an hour, finally giving up without catching one. I was glad we had hamburger in the refrigerator," I said.

Three hours later Bob and Arthur were back at the wharf, tying to the side of the '*Richard & Arnold*'. Much to our surprise, their skiff was loaded to the gunnels with mackerel. The boat was low in the water from the weight. They had smiles that went from ear to ear. Their young minds bubbling with enthusiasm, "Every time we put a hook in the water we hit a fish. I hope we make a pile of money." Robert said, "This must be where the saying, holy mackerel comes from." The two were exuberant, thinking about what they'd do with all their earnings. They did make some money, but not what they were expecting. They had two-hundred pounds of Mackerel and were paid twenty cents a pound for a grand total of $40.00. They split the money and Dave and I paid for their gas. Our son learned fish economics at an early age. We put the skiff away for the winter, but the next spring Dave and Robert were looking at bigger boats. As Robert grew so did his boats. He graduated from Massachusetts Maritime Academy in 2004 and now his boat is a one-hundred-eighty foot tugboat, the '*Yellow-Fin*'. Our family history in the fishing industry goes back generations but because of the limits placed on our business both our sons have set their courses away from fishing.

CHAPTER 9

Fishing with Friends

Many good people have gone fishing aboard the '*Richard &
Arnold*'. Family, friends and a few characters that deserve more
than just a few sentences, have crewed alongside Captain
Dave. Fishing isn't for everyone. It may seem adventurous
when you are sitting in an easy chair in front of the TV, but it
is hard work and it takes a special kind of person to keep at it.
When Dave finds a fellow who likes fishing, can do the work
and is easy to get along with - he scoops him up. A big fellow
from Maine named Warren turned up on the dock one day
looking for a job. Dave looked him in the eye and told him
he'd give him a trial run.

Warren was honest and told Dave he had problems at
home, needed a place to live and that he wanted to get his life
back on track. Dave took him fishing. He was strong, knew
what he was doing on the boat and was a good cook. Warren
moved aboard the '*Richard & Arnold*' that night and spent many
months living and working onboard. One morning Warren
and the captain were preparing for a fishing trip, "We've got

mice aboard," Warren told the captain. "Let's get a couple of mouse traps so I can sleep better." For this trip they needed a few groceries and a mouse trap so they headed to the local supermarket. When they returned to the boat our crewman said, "I'll put the foodstuff away and stow the gear. I'll be ready when you are." He went below to the foc'sle with the food.

The captain hollered to his crewman, "I forgot the flashlight batteries and we could use a couple pairs of gloves. Do you want to take a ride to the 'Lands' End Hardware' store with me?"

"Sure," Warren said and left the groceries on the table in the foc'sle. The two men headed up the wharf. They were gone half-an-hour, stopping to talk to Doc who worked in the marine supply section. When they came back to the boat Warren went below to finish putting the groceries away. A holler came from below deck, "Holy shit! Dave, come take a look at this!" The captain was in the foc'sle in a flash not knowing what to expect. They stared at the table. They were looking at what was left of the loaf of Wonder Bread; the plastic bag was empty and crumbs were swished across the table, like some kind of big tail had swept and dusted. There were just a few leftover crumbs. "Christ, I think we're going to need a bigger mouse trap. I don't think I can sleep down here anymore. That thing, whatever it is, is liable to haul me off to its den under the bunks." Warren was serious.

The captain told his crewman not to worry, "We'll get rid of it. Make some coffee and get ready to let the lines go."

It was a windy day with a swells four to six feet, the '*Richard &
Arnold*' did some rolling around out on the Stellwagen Bank.
There was the usual noise that always accompanies a dragger;
the engine roaring in the engine room, the winches screeching when hauling back, and the waves slapping sea against
the hull. Our small boat feels insignificant out there, but
she's sea-worthy. The motion is constant, she heaves and her
timbers shudder and the wood creaks as water surrounds the
boat. The day was spent hauling in and setting out the net.
Warren avoided the foc'sle as much as possible during the
eight hours they were gone. It had been a tiring day, the
catch was good and darkness had fallen when they headed in.
The men were happy when the lines were finally attached to
the poles at the pier.

Dave said, "It's late; let's unload the fish in the morning. If you can't sleep here you can come up the house with
me. I'm heading home." The captain went into the wheelhouse to shut down the lights and electronics. Warren sat on
the hatch of the fish-hold to remove his oil gear.

He looked up and yelled, "Hey, Cap! Quick! Look!"
There it was, illuminated by the light pole, making its way
up a rope and off the boat. A well fed varmint looking something like a big cat was moving back to dry land. It clung to
the hawser with muscle, teeth and claws. The animal hesitated at the top then turned its head and looked back as if it
wanted to remember not to hide there again. Two distinct
rings of black surrounding it eyes, like a thief in the night,
the animal looked pissed off, and then it hissed.

"Well I'll be," Warren said, "A ring-tailed raccoon. Just like a rat deserting a sinking ship. Good riddance to it," he said with a shudder, "Thank God it wasn't a rat. I hate rats."

The captain turned to his crewman, "I don't think we'll have to worry about seeing that fellow again. Something tells me he didn't like the life of a fisherman."

Warren laughed, "I don't think I'll mind sleeping here after all. See you in the morning." He headed for the foc'sle and Captain Dave headed home. Warren headed back to Maine the following autumn, sober and with money in his pocket.

A few weeks after Warren left, my husband brought home a young man who had just lost his driver's license, which led to his losing his job. Jimmy was big, strong and in need of direction, just the kind of crewman Dave liked to have working with him. He moved into our attic room and fished with Dave for over a year. Our two sons were too young for crew. Jackson helped out part time, during the summer and when he wasn't too busy with school, basketball or hockey. Robert was in grammar school and Jimmy became a part of the team and family.

Dave woke him at three o'clock every morning by yelling up the stairs, "Breakfast in fifteen minutes." Jimmy woke with enthusiasm, a smile on his face, looking forward to a day upon the water. This kind of life was new to him, he was learning about fishing, owning your own business and the wonders of the world. Jimmy was there the day the 'Richard & Arnold' had a 'floater' of Codfish. As the big net-reel turned it pulled the net onto a spool, bringing it up from the depths as the two men stood watching over the stern. Suddenly the net jumped from the water.

The young crewman wasn't sure what he was seeing, "Did you see that, Dave? The net is floating." As codfish rise to the surface, their bladders expand like bubbles causing the net to literally pop out of the water.

It means a great deal of work, for all the dead codfish have to be ripped and gutted, then washed, iced and stored. Jimmy was raring to put the net back over, so his enthusiasm was brought up short when he heard Dave holler across the deck, "Time to head in. We've got all we can handle."

Jimmy was ready to put the net back out, wanting more. Why would the captain stop when they were doing so well? Jimmy got his first taste of what it's like to rip and gut five thousand pounds of fish in one afternoon. At the end of three hours his wrists were swollen, his left hand that held the fish with two fingers inside the mouth or gill was stiff and painful. His right hand was cramped from holding the knife. To remove the guts, the knife cuts across the throat and down the belly, quickly. The parts not used are ripped from the inside and fed to the gulls and other fish. The fish are then washed, boxed and iced and when the box has one hundred pounds, it is lowered into the fish-hold. At the end of six hours all Jimmy wanted was to go home and sleep.

"Your wrist and hands will be sore for a couple of days. We don't get that kind of catch every day, so you'll have time to heal." Dave said. He was thinking that this young man was a natural on a boat. "And don't forget, hard work never killed a horse, just makes him sleep better."

"That boy is a keeper," Dave said after supper that night, "Like one of our sons. He's a big help, learns fast, a good crewman." Dave learned how much he cared about him the day we almost lost him on a foggy, cold, March afternoon. The boat had just come in from fishing in Nantucket Sound and Jimmy was on the bow with a line ready to tie up to a pole in Falmouth Harbor. The boat was moving slowly to the wharf and about to stop. As Jimmy stepped from the boat his wet boot slipped on the dock and into the water he went.

It happened fast, in a heartbeat, disaster. Dave backed down quickly then stopped the engine and hollered, hoping to attract attention from the men on other boats that were tied to the wharf. He yelled out, "Man overboard!" As loud as his voice would carry, "Man overboard!" Others heard and came running while Dave grabbed a boat hook and ran to the bow, hollering as he went, "Man overboard!"

Jimmy was flapping his arms, the heaviness and cold beginning to pull him down. Dave was able to grab the suspenders of Jimmy's oil gear with the boat hook, a twelve foot long pole, a gaff with a knobby hook on the end. Jimmy was sinking; the weight of his oil gear was so heavy that he could not keep himself up. Dave managed to stop the downward momentum and bring his head to the surface. "I've got you! Hang on! Kick off your boots, they fill with water and drag you down." Jimmy looked like Sesame Street's Big Bird, slowly pumping his yellow wings up and down. Fishermen from other boats arrived. Mike, Danny and Bobby brought a heavy line that had a loop tied into the end. Using all his strength, Dave held the pole hooked into Jim's suspenders, while Mike lowered the line into the water. "Put the rope around your waist." It took all four men to hoist the wet man to the safety of the deck.

"This is no time to go swimming, wait till the sun is shining," Dave held onto Jimmy as they walked to the foc'sle door. "You're going to need a new pair of boots. I'll take it out of your pay." Dave smiled. Jimmy chuckled and didn't care if it were true. Once into warm dry clothes, Jimmy began telling everyone he was fine and could help unload the boat. The captain told him he could have the rest of the day off. Dave made him soup, peanut butter sandwiches and hot tea, and then Jimmy crawled into his sleeping bag and slept like a baby. The next morning he was slightly embarrassed, but fit as a fiddle and wanting to go fishing. A useful lesson was learned that day: wait until the boat comes to a full stop, then, when all motion seems to cease, step gingerly from the boat. Somehow you'll know when a full stop is reached.

When Dave called home that night to tell me what had happened, he added, "He was heavy; I had all I could do to hold onto him. I don't know what would have happened if the others weren't there. Seeing him in the water made my heart stop. Thank God there were others there to help." Jimmy is now married with children and he still enjoys the watermen's life, growing clams and oysters, trapping lobsters, an independent fisherman.

The '*Richard & Arnold*' drags a net behind the boat for part of the year but we take trips for sea scallops as well. The permit that came with the boat when we bought her, allowed us to keep however many scallops we could catch. As with the *'Wildflower'*, the trips to the scallop ground offset the disappearance of the flat fish. The fish move, migrating, to live out the cold winter months. "Fish have tails," I have been reminded. Before record-keeping and cut off dates, before computer printouts and tracking devices, before quotas and catch shares, our boat caught tons of sea scallops.

Onboard for cold, rough rides to the scallop grounds can be an otherworldly experience. I happen to be one of many who get seasick. It has had a limiting effect on my days-at- sea. There is neither rhyme nor reason why some men get sea sick and some don't. I love being out there upon the water but only when there is not much motion, it may be the swells. I asked Dave why he never gets seasick. He said, "Because I have such a hard head."

Going fishing in winter with the air outside thick with moisture, slush appears on the deck. If the temperature is cold enough to freeze salt water and a wind builds up- it is as dangerous as it can get on the ocean. Tied to the dock is where you hope to be in that kind of weather. Yet, being out on the water when it snows is a great treat, big soundless snowflakes falling, disappearing into the water as snow surrounds the boat like a cocoon of white, the shore a half mile away, unseen, like I am on a tiny island, isolated inside a snow globe and I know why I love fishing.

Sea birds know when there is food. They appear as if by magic as soon as the scallop guts hit the water. They dive into the water after the entrails. In a matter of minutes the air is alive with them, swooping and diving. The birds look like they will plow into each other, but veer off to avoid collision, their wings pumping in a backward motion. A tug of war breaks out in front of my eyes, in midair, two gulls fight for the same piece of scallop remains. Screeches and sounds like human voices call out and I think I hear part of a word, or a call from someone far off. It is a sound of thank you and a staccato of joy.

A sea gull sat on the water watching as I stood at the rail in full yellow oil gear with Richard Dickey cutting scallops while the North wind howled around us. I had added heavy layers of clothing, a second pair of gloves, two pair of socks and insulated boots. Dickey had been sea scalloping or fishing for most of his life. He grew up in Wellfleet and began fishing before he left high school. We swapped stories, smoked cigarettes and cut fresh scallops into buckets as we stood at the rail. He told me about a boat he was crewing on that had a skipper who was always hollering out the window in Portuguese. It was his native language and the only language he apparently could speak. Richard laughed, "The captain was always yelling, hollering at us, pointing at things, but no one answered or seemed to obey his orders, or took any notice of him. He'd just shake his head and go back into the wheelhouse." Richard was chuckling, shoulders bobbing up and down, "It tuned out that not one person on the boat could speak Portuguese except the captain, and he couldn't understand us either. We all just did our job."

Shucking sea scallops starts with a plop-thunk, as the first meat hits the empty stainless-steel bucket. Like aroma therapy there is a rich smell of earth and sea combined with the sweet scent of scallop. The abductor muscle is all that we save, so the sea gulls and small fish were fed well. I love the gulls and watched as they pirouette while flapping their big grey and white feathers. Their calls reverberate against the waves, as music from a Puccini opera, a single voice touching heaven.

Richard Dickey has been called - a high-line shucker. He could open the bivalves faster than anyone we'd ever seen. He'd tell stories while we stood at the rail, his long lanky body in constant motion. He taught me to keep a hanky in my pocket, "The cold makes your nose run." He hoisted baskets full of scallops, dumping them into the wooden box that had been hastily nailed to the rail. We didn't stop talking. "The idea is to keep one shell in the air at all times." He made it seem effortless, like a juggler from the sea. We stood for hours, side by side, looking out at the water with knifes in hands. I listened when Richard talked about the time he got his jacket caught in the winch aboard a big scalloper out of New Bedford.

"Damn near killed me. Took me and spun me upside down, around and around, slamming me onto the deck with each rotation like being in a washing machine only worse." Richard was a gentleman and he never cursed in front of me. "That mother of a winch broke ribs, collarbone and a couple of bones in my arm. I was bruised in places I didn't know I had. It took months to recover."

"Watch out around the winches, young lady," he warned. His stories, advice and views of life were well worth the aches and pains of standing ten hours in the freezing cold. He was a spiritual man who had a wonderful sense of his place in the universe. His humor touched all who met him, and of coarse the pot he smoked made him very philosophical. We spoke of Enoch and the Dead Sea Scrolls as well as crazy trips to the fishing grounds with captains who couldn't speak English.

Sea Scallops kept a fleet of boats busy working from Provincetown Harbor. The *'Terra Nova'*, the *'Katherine Marie'*, the *'Cape Star'*, the *'Alwa'*, the *'Josephine G'*, the *Richard & Arnold'* and many others brought scallops back to Provincetown from miles off shore. The captains of the boats usually had piles of sea scallops in the hold ready to be opened. They made phone calls looking for people who wanted to earn money shucking for a couple of days. Sometimes as many as twenty people worked the deck, while the boat stood at anchor in the harbor. There seemed to be a never ending supply of scallops.

Men talked, shucked, smoked, slept and ate their meals in the foc'sle. The crews worked steadily: cutting, washing and bagging, filling the cutter's area with bivalves until the hold was empty. The uniform shells fit into the palm of my hand, each with razor sharp edges. Thick rubber gloves kept my hands safe and warm while I filled a 10-quart bucket, eight times in a day. The shucker's wage, not crew, was $10 per bucket and enough to make any temporary help - happy. At the end of twelve hours the crews went home tired, but always willing to do it again tomorrow. Some nights I'd sleep in my long underwear, not able to raise my arms over my head, "Hard work never killed a horse," Dave said, "Just makes him sleep better." I'd tell Dave to shut up, I'd heard that before.

Being out upon the ocean when the winds howl and swells build, is something I wouldn't wish on anyone. It is a humbling experience. Up over crests of crashing curls, rocking, falling into a swell, a dot upon the water, feeling the ocean's force, knowing how insignificant you are, while slowly making headway toward safe harbor. The motion is different depending upon the direction you are heading, in relation to the direction of the wind, current and tide. Downwind is not so bad, the boat heaves slightly and the motion although constant, is not one of crashing. It's having her timbers shudder when heading into curling surf that gives me a scary feeling. When I feel the first ten feet of the boat come off the top of a wave and pound into the trough of the next, feeling weightless, I hang on with arms and legs, or rest in a bunk as my body lifts slightly off the mattress.

Sitting in his chair in the tiny wheelhouse, Dave bites the bottom edge of his mustache, intent on some unseen force. He watches the movement of the waves and compensates just so slightly while running down a swell. The boat responds to the motion with grace. The 'Richard & Arnold' has surfed down swells and has rolled around for eighty years, while steaming or towing in all sorts of weather. When there is a small window of time in which the weather cooperates and there are no unforeseen problems, he takes the boat and goes fishing. Our family fishing history began before we bought the 'Richard &

Arnold' and the boat's fishing history dates to 1927 before permits were first issued. The boat is one of a kind and she's still doing what she was built for.

Dave prefers dragging a net to dragging a rake. Fishing is easier on the boat, the crew and the captain. The fish come and go in cycles and seasons. Fluke season is great because everything is better in summer. Yellow-tail flounders are caught near home in the fall and are his wife's favorite eating fish. Cod-fish come to the middle bank during certain months but they can be very elusive. Whiting fishing is hard, it requires lots of help, the fish are cheap and it is only with tonnage that you make money. Squid means leaving home for weeks, but by the spring everyone is hungry. Sea scallops fill the void when fish move. Scallops don't move much, they are filter feeders and as long as the area has food, they remain fairly stationary, although they can move five feet with one clap of their shells. Dave and I have learned the advantages and disadvantages of the seasons and cycles of nature. We had to learn how to deal with the ups and downs of the business. And then, we had to learn how to deal with the complications that arose as many agencies began appearing, expanding and regulating.

Whether on placid sunny days or in sloppy wet seas, many people have fished aboard the *'Richard & Arnold'*. Some stay for a year or months and some come for the day to see what fishing is about. Our friend Krissy loves to be out on the water and goes fishing whenever she can, to get away from the stresses in her life and live care-free for a few hours. She is a spiritual and creative person, unconventional, a nonconformist and loves a day of sun. In August the weather is calm and hot, a good time to get away from it all, so when she asked Dave if she could spend the day out fishing with him, he agreed.

Dave's crewman that summer was a fellow named Paul. There was enough fish being caught to warrant extra help and Paul needed to be away from the temptations on land. He was an experienced deckhand, had lots of energy and would help out wherever needed. "He can scramble up the ladder like a monkey and the foc'sle has never been so clean." Dave liked his crew neat. The two men would keep an eye on Krissy.

There is a small triangular place half way up the main mast that has a piece of net tied into it, like a hammock or a nest. Krissy had made herself at home up there. She had her water color paints, a book and some lunch. There is a feeling that you sometimes get when out on the water, one that I can relate to, a feeling of freedom - like you are alone in the world. The calm and warmth combine to produce a relaxed atmosphere, so nature loving Krissy removed her shirt. Needing a break she climbed down and was at the rail in hat, shorts and boots, opening a scallop shell when Paul came out of the foc'sle with a plate of food for the captain and walk right past Krissy.

Paul kept his head and eyes straight ahead, stiff, like a soldier. When he got to the wheelhouse his eyes were open wide. "Jesus Christ! What the f— are you trying to do to me, Cap?" He handed the plate of food to Dave and said, "I just got out of jail, how much you think I can take?"

Krissy heard his voice clearly. Turning, she said in a very sweet voice, "Oh, I am so sorry" and produced a shirt from the backpack she'd left on deck. The atmosphere on the boat became more relaxed. Paul gave everyone a grin and went back below decks to make the captain a cup of tea to go with his lunch. Krissy went up to her nest.

Later that same day Dave came out of the wheelhouse and told Paul, "Looks like we are going to have to go in early. We've got a bad shake in the wheel. I think a rope is caught in the propeller."

Paul was quick to reply, "I can help you. I wouldn't mind going over the side and cutting the line out for you, cap. It's a nice day for a swim." During this little conversation Krissy perched above the deck, sunning, reading and eating crackers with cheese from a can is unaware of what is happening below. Krissy is unseen and forgotten. With the engine out of gear, the boat drifts, hardly moving. Paul steps out of his clothes and took a knife from Dave.

Before you could say 'Marlinspike Sailor' he was over the side and into the cold clear water. Krissy felt the change in motion. She rolls out of her little nest, climbed down and asked, "What's going on?" Dave tells her that Paul is taking line out of the wheel so that they can keep fishing. They lean over the side to watch and wait. A minute passes and then the skinny white body of the buccaneer - a knife between his teeth - surfaces. He hisses, "Get her out of here, Dave, and get her below. Don't let her see me like this." He is clinging to a rope like a monkey.

Krissy laughs a high pitched bubble and tells Paul, "I'm leaving. Don't flatter yourself; you've got nothing I haven't already seen."

"You don't understand. This is very cold water. No Fair." Krissy climbed back up the mast and Dave hauled Tarzan out of the water. With the line out of the wheel they continued fishing. The rest of the day flew by without another incident. Krissy stayed stretched out in the little crow's nest all but forgotten as the men picked through the pile at the end of each tow. The mast swings slowly like a cradle, the boat rolls and Krissy fell asleep. Later that afternoon there is a change in sound and motion, then a small thump against the wharf, waking Krissy from her nap. She sits up.

Dave brought the boat alongside Fishermen's Wharf and Krissy is now eye level with two guys, lumpers, who are going to unload the catch to the fish buyer. She is topless again. The guys on the wharf begin to applaud. She bows and tilts her head like an actress on the stage and slips into her shirt. The men are tripping over each other to get Dave's lines. Krissy gives everyone smiles as she gathers up her picnic and heads for the deck.

The boat was tied in its berth and Dave was walking to get his truck when he saw Captain Louie, of the '*Miss Sandy*' who has been fishing in the same area all day. Louie gives Dave a 'big thumbs up' and says, "That's some crew you have there. We've been watching her all day. Didn't catch much fish but we sure had a good time." Then Louie made a barking sound, "Ruff, Ruff."

I received a phone call before Dave walked in the kitchen door. I was told that there was a naked woman on the boat all day. I stuttered then said thank you and hung up. I said nothing when Dave came in tired and hungry. I was quiet during supper. I asked about his day and he told me the fishing wasn't good -only five boxes, they'd had a line in the wheel, but everything was fine. Later, as Dave was falling asleep I asked, "Is it true that there has been a naked woman on the boat all day?"

Dave sat up, sputtering, "Who told you that? It's not completely true, and Paul was onboard, and I hardly saw a thing, and she was up in the rigging all day." I frowned and he started to laugh, really laugh, hard with tears in his eyes and said, "What a wild and crazy day." I got the whole story between laughter and apologies. I called Krissy the next day and ask her, as a friend, to keep her clothes on when she was out on the boat. I told her, "I get jealous." She always did after that, but at the next 'Provincetown Blessing of the Fleet' Krissy gave us all a surprise.

The shirt was a beige sleeveless tee and Krissy used her great artistic ability to paint the chest of a mermaid on it, two big beautiful breasts. She'd kept her word and kept a shirt on. She sat in the rigging, as she had before, appearing naked. Thousands of people lined the wharf to watch the parade of boats. The Bishop from the New Bedford Archdiocese blessed the fleet. When our turn came, we passed in front of the pier. Cheering, hollering and applause came from the spectators as I rang the ship's bell and Dave sounded the horn. The crowd yelled louder. We'll never know if the acclaim was for our old fishing boat or for the tee shirt Krissy wore. Bless her heart - she is a true artist and a true friend. She knows how to have fun and best of all — isn't afraid to express herself.

The ups and downs in this business are just part of the job. Whether summer days with Krissy onboard or working windy October afternoons off the Highland Lighthouse, fishing the *'Richard & Arnold'* is never dull. One day crewman Peter Morris after clearing the deck of fish stepped into the wheelhouse and said, "Man, I'm soaked. I'm going below to change and make us something hot to eat." Dave nodded and watched Pete disappear into the foc'sle. After half an hour, Dave checked the radar again, not one blip, no other boats or markers, so he set the autopilot and went below to see if lunch was ready. As he descended the ladder in boots and oil gear Peter said to him, "It sure is rough out there."

"It's not rough, just a little rock and roll," Dave jammed his body between the wall and table while Peter braced himself and gave the captain a bowl of fish stew.

"Rock and roll?" Peter pointed to the top of the ladder, out through the foc'sle door toward the steely grey sky. "Not rough? What do you call that?"

David turned and watched as a wave came up behind the boat, rising six feet over the top of the wheelhouse, while the boat towed the net gently down the swell. Both men realized it was time to head in. Dave said, "A bit more than I thought. Looks like this will be our last tow tonight. Let's head in." The catch that one tow was over a thousand pounds of yellow tail flounder, lobsters and monk fish and they wanted to do it again, but knew it was time to leave. Dave is fond of a Clint Eastwood expression, "A man's got to know his limitations." They rounded Race Point, along the Wood End and into the harbor just in time to leave a raging northeast storm in their wake. They were the only boat out that day and the fish brought the highest prices at the auction that week. Dave tells me it was worth a little rock and roll. In all kinds of weather, rain or snow, calm or rough, cold or warm, Dave and his friends have loved every minute of fishing. These men and women have brought good cheer, good help and good fish to our home, our town, our community, our area, our cape and our world. The saying 'fishing rhymes with wishing not catching' is a clear indication that many of our fishing friends are dreamers, thinkers, philosophers as well as men of action and independence. Fishing with crewmen is good, fishing alone is sometimes necessary, but fishing with friends is the best.

CHAPTER 10

Fishing Assistance

Dave and I have the utmost respect for the United States Coast Guard. They come when you call, risk their own and save many lives. We who go about the waterways are thankful for their efforts and we salute them. We also know that man is not born upon the sea and must learn to live with, on and around it. And so the few stories regarding mishaps and misunderstandings appearing here should be taken with a grain of salt.

"Every day out fishing is a story," Dave reminds me. "At three in the morning I had just entered the harbor and could see our mooring about a hundred yards off, when out of the dark night, blue lights flashed across the water." Dave recalls his day as we sit with cups of tea at the kitchen table. "From a loudspeaker, a hand held megaphone, I am told to take the boat out of gear and be prepared to be boarded." Being boarded by the local Coast Guard is an experience similar to being stopped on the highway by a state trooper- you hope everything is in order.

Dave continued, "I cut the engine and turned on the deck lights. A thirty foot cutter came alongside. A young fellow stepped onto my rail and proceeded to tie their boat to the '*Richard & Arnold*'. A few words of greeting were exchanged and the Officer in charge asked to see my papers and to see my fish. I showed him where the fish are kept in the tubs on deck and he and his men began counting and measuring every fish, taking them from the cold water, then putting them in boxes. I was alone on the boat and had about three thousand pounds of mixed fish on board." Dave paused in the narration, "I asked the officer in charge if we could, please, tie up to the town dock or to my mooring so I could turn off the engine. I'd been listening to it for eighteen hours and I was tired.

"No Sir" was the answer.

"Maybe they thought you were smuggling contraband like drugs, guns, or illegal aliens?" I suggested.

Dave gave me a tired smile, "The chief looked over all my licenses while his men measured the fish, every single fish. We drifted and moved around for over an hour, just yards from the dock, feet from my mooring. I'm proud to say there was not one illegal sized fish on board. The Coast Guard was out for a night practice run. Night time maneuvers are required training." Dave sighed, "Some people think that fishermen are not honest, I worry that fishing has been branded as a bad thing."

David and I have always thought of ourselves as honest people, but a few years ago an incident took place that made us feel like criminals. Dave went fishing, taking along two men with slightly notorious backgrounds. Paul had recently been released from the Barnstable House of Correction -something to do with drugs- but he was clean. He is a good deck hand and the fish were running. He's the same skinny kid with red hair and wild look in his eyes that went over the side, naked, with a knife in his teeth, when Krissy was on board.

Dean, the other crewman was a friend who had fished his own boat at one time, but had problems with women, booze and drugs. Dean, over six feet tall with dark hair and dark eyes is handsome enough to be in a TV commercial. Good help comes and goes in the fishing business and because these guys knew how to handle themselves on a boat, they stayed on as crew, knowing that no drugs or alcohol are allowed on our boat. Dave recalled the night, "The fish hold contained ten thousand pounds. Everyone was tired but happy with the catch. It was dark when blue lights appeared out of nowhere. An officer with a megaphone was standing on the Cutter's rail and hailed us, "Prepare to be boarded." The sea was choppy with a small swell. The '*Richard & Arnold*' rolled slightly, but the cutter was bouncing like a cork in a bathtub. The movement between the boats was not coordinated, but disjointed like mismatched partners at a dance. There seemed to be static in the air, as if a storm was building strength. With the deck lights on, the boat was an island in the dark."

David sighed and continued, "The quick fiberglass vessel was bobbing and bouncing alongside the heavier, slower '*Richard & Arnold*' creating a haphazard motion. My crewmen were in good moods, so this routine was just an annoying stop."

I snuggled closer to Dave as he continued, "I've been through this kind of stop- search, count, observed or checked- so many times it's just time out of my day. Two young uniformed men step lively onto the railing of the *'Richard & Arnold'* and they are carrying what looks like machine guns strapped over their shoulders."

I sat up to listen more attentively, "The air felt ominous," Dave continued. "I moved my head from side to side, watching the men with guns and then my two crewmen. Dean in oil gear is coming out from the doghouse in the bow. He looks like he's seven feet tall in boots and yellow slicker. While Paul, our wild man, is standing mid-ship. The Coast Guardsman pointed his gun toward Paul and yelled with all the authority he can muster, "SIT DOWN. I SAID SIT DOWN.""

Dave gave a short shudder, "Paul begins to move forward, toward the Coast Guard crewman, slowly, hunched, creeping. The serviceman is standing on the rail of the *'Richard & Arnold'* and because there is a noticeable difference in motion, the young man begins rocking, waving the gun from side to side. For a minute we all thought he was going to fall into the water, then he staggered and leaned onto a stay wire and with all the confidence he could assume, he screams again at Paul, "SIT DOWN!" His knuckles look white against the black sky."

Now Dave is smiling, "My deckhand apparently doesn't give a shit about authority. He stands up and screams back at the twenty year old guardsman with the gun, "YOU DON'T TELL ME WHAT TO DO ON THIS BOAT - IF MY CAPTAIN

TELLS ME TO JUMP UP THERE AND RIP YOUR HEART
OUT THROUGH YOUR THROAT, THAT'S JUST WHAT
I'LL DO."

"The young officer stood motionless, stricken, para-
lyzed, and unsure of what to do next." David stopped the
story and started to laugh until tears were rolling down his
cheeks. I am horrified.

He continued, "I stepped from the wheelhouse with
palms face up, into the night sky and as calmly as possible I
said, "hold on, hold on" in a way that would give everyone
on board time to regroup their thoughts. I quietly said, "No
need of this Paul. Sit down!" Paul backed to the other rail with
a mischievous grin on his face and at that moment I know this
really is a joke to him."

Dave had to stop laughing to finish his story, "You
could cut the air with a knife, then everyone seemed to take
a breath as Paul sits on the rail, grinning. There was a visible
difference in everyone's attitude. I produced my paper work
out of my old briefcase; a young officer checked the fish hold
very quickly, the grey totes were examined but no fish were
removed and in less than fifteen minutes the local unit is back
aboard the cutter and gone."

"At first my motley crew is just smiling and I was shaking
my head. Then Paul puts on a sheepish grin and his shoulders
are bobbing up and down. He's laughing and Dean is laughing and then I'm laughing along with them." I said nothing;
I didn't think it was funny. All of the 'what-ifs' were running
through my mind. Just before he fell asleep Dave said, "I'm

not kidding when I tell you that had to be one of the scariest things I've ever had to deal with aboard the boat."

The world around the water is filled with joy, beauty, mystery and sometimes frightening things. When things happen, they happen fast. On a warm summer night in August the wind was blowing from the prevailing direction of southwest. In Provincetown it is not uncommon for wind speeds to exceed forty knots across the open harbor. On this particular evening the wind felt heavy with coming rain. The '*Richard & Arnold*' was secured at her berth while Dave and I walked around the waterfront hand in hand. We followed the bulkhead, meandering, looking out across Provincetown harbor. We had the long summer twilight to see by. We heard the noisy, splashing sounds of water slapping against the floats and then the roar of an engine revving its motor that drew our attention to a scene directly below us.

Tied broadside to a cement float was a white fiberglass boat with an orange stripe down the bow. This boat was trying to get away from the dock, to turn its bow up into the strong southwest wind. Everything happened fast. Dave was flying through the air onto the platform 5 feet below us. In an instant there was chaos.

A Coast Guardsman was attempting to push the bow of the boat up into the wind, away from the wharf, using his body weight to push against the boat. He slipped and suddenly found himself in the water between the boat and the concrete floating pier. Dave, not stopping to think, knowing something had to be done immediately, landed on the deck of the moving platform, while I sat on the wall staring at this incredible scene, feeling helpless. Dave grabbed the young man by the back of his shirt and literally yanked him, in one full motion, out of the water, from in-between the smashing moving masses. The men on the boat did not see their shipmate go into the water.

The soaked young man was coughing and sputtering as he sat on the thrashing dock. Without saying a word he was trying to light a cigarette from a package he took from his wet shirt pocket. Dave meanwhile, was hollering to the men on the vessel to set a spring-line, an additional line that will assist the boat to pull the bow away by keeping the stern toward the dock. The wet young man got up and moved with sober intent. He never said one word to David as he climbed aboard the rocking fiberglass vessel. The line was sprung, the boys waved to us and the boat headed its nose into the southwest wind with all safely aboard. As they moved away, I wrapped my arms around Dave, "My hero! You're a take control kind of a guy and I'll bet that young man is glad you were here tonight, at just the right moment."

We are currently on an even keel with our neighbors and helpers, the USCG. We are boarded at least once a year and we have dockside inspections for safety. The captains and crews are required to carry photo identification, a mandatory fishing vessel operator's permit. I think it's for the better, because with Dave's Portugese ancestry he could easily be mistaken for an Arab, or Asian, or Mexican or Haitian, maybe a Phoenician or Greek or even a Portugese fisherman.

Fishermen have a reputation of being the 'bad-boy' type and many are. A young coast guard officer told me a story about what took place on one of our fishing draggers in 1980. There were rumors circulating that a few of the sixty boats that called Provincetown home were smuggling contraband into town. The Coast Guard was keeping a close eye on the comings and goings of boats from the harbor. Pot was high on the list of illegal substances thought to be smuggled because it was being smoked all over town. One night the '*Zerta*' was just rounding the tip of Cape Cod coming back to Provincetown, when the Coast Guard stopped the boat and proceeded to board. Captain Joe, with black bushy beard and wild hair, looking like Black-Bart, the pirate, stepped from the wheelhouse and welcomed the uniformed men aboard. He told them he was heading in early because he had had some engine trouble and they didn't catch any fish. The officer in charge sent two men to check the fish pens in the boat's deep hull. Down the twelve-foot ladder into the bowels of the boat, the young men went. One naked light bulb hung from a four foot cord at the center of the long cement aisle. It was damp and cold and the floor vibrated with the rumbling of the engine. The men walked half way down the cement path seeing a clean fish-hold. There was ice in the forward pens, but no fish. The boat appeared empty after a cursory inspection. Being satisfied that all was as Joe had told them, the young men made their way back up the ladder. Just as the last man stepped to the deck he heard a sneeze. Unsure of the noise, he turned around to have a second look. Was that a body? The uniformed young man felt his heart jump. He saw a hand, then an arm and next a man's head. Then out from under the ice people began to emerge. They had been covered by a tarp and were unseen in the dingy light.

A holler went up to the Chief Mate, "Sir, come take a look at this." A group of Haitian men, twelve in all, were hiding in the forward fish pens. When Joe and his crew saw the flashing blue lights on the water, they shoveled ice on top of tarps covering the smuggled people. The boat was confiscated. Everyone was arrested, eventually Joe had to serve time and the illegal immigrants were deported. Yet, the best part of the story came the night after the arrest while Joe was out on bail. He showed up at the wedding reception of his cousin who was marrying the same Coast Guard officer who arrested him. "No hard feelings," Joe told the groom. "I know you were just doing your job."

The local constabulary now recognizes the individual boats in our area and they know we are glad they are here. They safeguard the sea, but their role has changed over the years. Today the USCG has to count fish, check papers, watch the coast for shady looking boats, keep track of sightings of northern right whales, and keep illegal immigrants along with illegal fish from flooding our supermarkets, besides saving the lives of boaters from all walks of life. The Coast Guardsmen put their lives on the line to help those in distress and for that we are in their debt. And yet there are times when not even the Coast Guard can be there in time.

The sea scallop fishery began to change after we lost seven Provincetown men in one night as they returned from the scallop grounds. The *'Patricia Marie'* with Captain Billy King and his crewmen were experienced fishermen. They had made the trip many times in all kinds of weather. The water is cold in October. Any number of things can go wrong. Pumps can stop working, a plank in the hull can come loose, seas over the bow can break away an unlocked hatch, the boat can hit a sand bar, or the rake may slip from the deck and the boat rolls over. A boat can sink in minutes. It doesn't matter what the cause - it only matters that the children, wives, mothers and fathers, brothers, sisters, cousins and friends will never see their men again.

Two years later, on a freezing February night, the *'Captain* Bill' slipped into the deep somewhere off the Highland of Truro with Captain Andrews and his three crewmen onboard. People gathered on the wharf talking quietly in groups, shaking their heads, wondering what had gone wrong as they waited for word from the U.S. Coast Guard, but nothing was ever found.

Provincetown mourned the loss of three young men who had yearned for the sea with the sinking of the 'Victory' which now rests near the Billingsgate buoy. The knowledge that the sea can call us home at any time is a bond of all men working the open water. The 'Sol-a-Mar', the 'Lonely Hunter' and the 'Cathy B' with crewmen, family men, fishermen all, were taken to sleep with Neptune's daughters. When a fishing vessel is lost at sea it is felt by every person who makes their living from the ocean. Ask any fishermen and he'll tell you he knows the risks, but that he'd rather be fishing than any other job on earth.

It has always been my fear, a great weight, a dark thought in the shadows of my mind - that someday it could be my boat, my husband and my sons. Still we go out upon the sea to make a living. We are ever mindful of the majesty and power that surrounds us. It is never taken for granted and we are continually thankful for its bounty and for the help of the United States Coast Guard.

CHAPTER 11

Fishing with Uncle Sam

This statement appears on page twenty-three of the 1988 "Fishing Vessel Safety, Blueprint for a National Program" - A comprehensive assessment by the National Academies of Sciences and Engineering, "Fishermen are often viewed by social observers as a quaint sub-culture group displaying special social and cultural qualities: individualism, carefree, rugged, self-sufficient and in some cases fatalistic. Fishermen more frequently characterize themselves as hunters." The fishermen I have known are not fatalistic. They know what has to be done aboard their vessel. They don't throw caution to the wind. They are practical, in control of their own destinies and they have a great sense of humor, as a sub-culture that is. My definition, evaluation and classification of fishermen most likely is a little different from the one recorded in the blueprint. I find them to be free-spirited, hardworking, independent and spiritual.

The fishing methods used here in Provincetown haven't changed much over the past eighty years but the master plan of who will control the taking of fish has changed the fishery completely. With the consolidation of the fishery many coastal communities throughout the northeast have lost whole fleets of fishing boats, businesses and families.

Fifty years ago the nets that were dragged from the boats out of Provincetown harbor had a one-inch mesh size. They caught everything. This brought about the tragic and terrible decline in the fish. Intervention in the 1980's by federal and state regulators increased the mesh sizes. First three inch-mesh, then four inch, then four and one half then eventually regulations called for a six-inch mesh size on all ground fishing, dragging or otter-trawl nets. We were throwing away nets every year at our own expense, but this one change in method has caused a great leap forward toward a sustainable fishery. The increase in mesh size means that fish caught today are past the juvenile stage. Of course you never know what else will be mixed in with the catch no matter what size the mesh. We shovel over: mud, broken bottles, sticks, sea weed, carcasses of half eaten fish, empty shells, uneatable sea cucumbers, crabs, starfish, piles of broken wood that used to be a lobster trap (ghosters, they're called) crushed soda cans, piles of unwanted wire line used by the rod and reel recreational fishermen, old gill nets and long lines with hooks, an odd assortment of rubber gloves, rocks, empty artillery shells, anchors, glass bottles, tires, parts of someone's deck and staircases washed away in storms, parts of sunk boats, plastic bags, mussels, tree trunks, branches and other junk not so pleasant.

During one tow just south of Martha's Vineyard the *'Ann Marie'* was hauling back the net when it snagged an unexploded torpedo from WWII. The bomb exploded underwater while the net was being dragged toward the boat. It blew out the wheelhouse windows and melted the net buoys. Thank heaven no one was hurt. Another year a fishing boat in Cape Cod Bay dragged up barrels of some unknown chemical that made everyone on board sick. The debris comes in on currents, perhaps thrown overboard, perhaps dumped from barges ten years ago, or maybe they are storm driven from the shore. One year a container vessel heading for Boston Harbor dropped a cargo box overboard in heavy seas and for weeks afterward small dolls were washing up on Truro's shores. We never know what will be in the net.

In order to put the net in the water today there is a piece of paper for every fish you can catch. Fish size, the amount of fish allowed to be kept, where you can go to fish, how much time you are allowed to fish are just a few of the regulations that have affected the fleets. There is no fishing allowed inside 3 miles one hour after sunset to one hour before sunrise - the nautical twilight hours. For months at a time we are shut out of fishing around the cape due to 'rolling closures'. If we fish in the Gulf of Maine we are charged two hours for every one hour of allotted time. When Dave and I discuss these changes to our fishery he says, "What part of - *we don't want you here* — don't you understand." He repeats this to me when the notices come.

We receive letters regarding regulations from National Marine Fisheries Service on a daily basis. It makes it difficult to make a business plan. Dave and I can't figure out what path to take because we don't know what will come next. For me, the idea of our own government putting us out of business has always been unbelievable, something foreign, and un-American. During the early 1990's federally permitted fishing vessels were each given a total of 88 days-at-sea in which to catch fish. Most felt that it was equitable and fair. Yet more fishing boats left the industry because they were unable to catch enough in that time frame to make it profitable. Eighty-eight days was good for us, we made a good living because Dave could still bring in what he caught.

It was during the 1990's, while no one was paying attention, that a line was drawn on a chart by a well-meaning Federal Judge at the urging of the National Marine Fisheries Service - on behalf of the NE Fishery Council- that closed our traditional fishery down. This ruling meant that off the coast of Chatham, MA, a thirty five mile car drive around the peninsular to our south — a fisherman could land two-thousand pounds (2,000) of codfish per day. The boats fishing north of the line were allowed thirty (30) pounds per day. For those who get into their car and drive from Provincetown to Chatham this doesn't seem like much of a hardship. We could take our old boat during the winter months - below this 42nd degree line, taking three to four hours to get there, fish and hope we catch something, praying no problems arise — then we would be allowed to take two-thousand pounds for the day.

The small boats out of Chatham Harbor jumped at the chance of making money during the winter months using gill nets and long lines with hooks. They could set the stationary nets during calm weather, run back to harbor while the gillnets fished in place and then when the weather cooperated, run back out to collect their nets and fish. It worked for them-they began accumulating a large catch history during the years 1996 to 2006. When this line was drawn we had no idea that our catch history for Codfish was at stake.

I have nothing against the hard working fishermen from Chatham; I admire their skill and devotion to fishing. But it must be understood that this demarcation line gave the Chatham fishermen an unfair advantage in the government's management plan. The Chatham Hook Fishermen's Association then received a special access area, an unprecedented benefit, and an unequal share of fish profit when it came time to 'allocate'. I can only wonder at the coincidence that the chairman of the New England Fishery Council also sat on the board of directors of the Chatham Fishermen's Association. The Council's job is to make proposals regarding regulations to the National Marine Fisheries Service. Unfortunately no one from Provincetown sits on the New England Fishery Council; we do not have college graduates running our co-op. We are fishermen.

Chatham got special access while Provincetown's catch history was disallowed. 'Control dates' were established for a boat's total catch history -using the years 1996 to 2006 - to gift out allocation by NMFS. Provincetown's fleet got nothing — having landed only thirty pounds of cod per day — while the gillnetters from Chatham got the largest allocations of anyone in the northeast.

Where is our moral indignation, our outrage? How does the government justify this action? Where have American democracy, decency and fairness gone?

Our eighty year old boat has survived because it has been properly maintained and because it was never treated recklessly. A trip to Grand Banks in winter would be as stupid as would a run down the backside of the Cape in December to catch codfish. There's fish here, close to home, but we're not allowed to catch them. Where once we could fish as nature allowed, now we are permitted by agencies. Where once we could schedule our own days of fishing, now we are allotted 'day-at-sea' to fish for ground fish. Much of our local fishing history is lost for all time, never to be recovered. Ice-houses, hundreds of wharfs, thousands of boats and Scully-Joes have disappeared from my mirror. Scully-Joes are small cod fish soaked for days in salt brine then hung on clothes lines in the back yard to dry. They are a tradition that has not survived the changes to the fishery. The scrod cod are now an illegal size fish. There are only a few people left in Provincetown who know how to make them.

Not long ago the '*Charlotte*' was cut up for scrap, the last open dory-boat that fished the weirs in Cape Cod Bay from the 1930's to the 1960's. There were many fish traps, stationary nets called weirs, situated around the bay and boats like the '*Charlotte*' worked them. It was an industry that used manpower to pull in the nets. Weir fishing disappeared as the draggers took over the fishing industry. The *"Charlotte'* went by the 'ways', slipping from sight, with only a note of remembrance, a small article in the local newspaper, wrenching our hearts. She was an authentic, tangible piece of history that is gone for all time. The same thing is happening throughout the small fishing communities from Maine to Florida.

The National Marine Fisheries Service implemented the 'calling in and out' system and I was upset by the idea that Dave could not leave the dock to go fishing without making a phone call to Big Brother first. When this system was initiated we had to pay for the call, usually in Kansas or Utah. I had a hard time understanding why this regulation was put in place until a couple of years later, when the feds began allocating the fishery by the number of days or the amount of time in hours - or 'effort' - you put into it. Unfortunately nothing about fishing is ever on an even keel and effort is a relative phrase. Someone decided that the time you spent fishing would be the basis for an equation to limit access to fishing days. So that if you didn't fish much- you got 'not much'. If you left your clock running all the time as some men did (calling in but not calling out) - even if they were <u>not</u> out fishing - you got lots and lots of days. If you were ill or had some other problems and didn't use your boat to fish - you got nothing. There are many reasons boats can't get out fishing: weather, breakdowns, electronic problems, crews don't show up, illness, and family problems, just to mention a few. The fewer days spent out upon the sea- the fewer days you were allocated

- none of it based on equality. As always, the bigger the boat, the more time you were able to put in.

'Allocation' has been one of the nails used to close the coffins on many fishing businesses. Allocations reward the biggest efforts, leaving the little guy scratching his head wondering what happened. Most fishermen in Provincetown changed the type of fishing gear they used at different times of the year - from fishing to scalloping, clamming or lobstering, taking the effort from one area and placing it in another. Fishing boats would come in and out of fishing on a regular basis, but the big machine of government just kept right on rolling, spewing out more directives. We were told to put effort into other areas. We switched to sea scallop aquaculture, hoping to develop a different way to make money. We felt we were doing our part by taking the pressure off the fish populations. It had been pounded into us that there were not enough fish out there and it was up to us to make changes. We did our part by fishing less and exploring other avenues. We were punished for it in the end. The years spent researching sea scallop aquaculture counted as zero work days in the fishery — no effort — less hours equals less allocation.

Here in Provincetown we are losing the last of our kind. The eastern-rigged dragger is becoming extinct. I was walking on the wharf behind a man and woman not long ago and I heard the man say, "I remember when this wharf was filled with fishing boats tied to the pier, four and five deep. I remember when the trucks hauling fish off the pier numbered fifteen in a day." The man shook his head. "Now I hear they are closing the high school because there are no families left in town. I know that fishing families filled the schools when I lived here." They walked away, his words ringing in my ears. I wanted to cry.

The latest in the thirty-five year history of the Magnuson/Stevens Act is Amendment 16, Framework 42 of the Small Entity Compliance Guide. It is so restrictive that it is impossible to continue to make a living at fishing. Under the new regulations if our '*Richard & Arnold*' does not join a sector and wants to fish in the Gulf of Maine, our boat will have 16 days to fish. Each day we are allowed 100 pounds of cod fish, 250 pounds of yellowtail flounder, a smattering of by-catch and <u>no</u> flounder at all, we'll have to throw them overboard dead. Someone told me that the government has no heart, has no soul and that no one is responsible. From what I have witnessed, I am beginning to think that might be true.

If the purpose is to eliminate older, smaller, more vulnerable fishing businesses, then the NMFS has injured by prejudice – the men and women who caught less than the new arrivals into the fishing industry – rewarding those who pushed the hardest during the period of time - 1999-2006. If I were in charge my proposal would be to change the control dates to reflect a different criteria - all those who held licenses between 1980 and 1990 step forward, it's an arbitrary pick of years. I'd like to hear the men who have literally put the small draggers out of business holler, "that's not fair."

Under Amendment 16 of the Sustainable Fisheries Act – '<u>Sector Management</u>' - is created. On top of the new rules and regulation, Fisher-folk will still need to keep up with the following which are already in effect:

Recordkeeping & Reporting

Gear Restrictions

Exemptions

Days at Sea

Days-At-Sea Declaration and Accounting

Time /Area Closures

Minimum Commercial Fish Size

US / Canadian Management Areas

Closed Areas

Special Access Programs: Winter Flounder SAP, Yellow tail SAP, Haddock SAP

Possession and Landing Limits

Hand Gear Permits

Open Access Permits

Recreational Measures

Dave and I have never questioned our choice to make our living from the sea. Maybe we should have sold our permit years ago, when it still had value, but then we would never be able to go fishing again. It would mean we give up the right to fish and I don't think we are willing to do that. Today those same pieces of paper that we fought to hang on to, are just about worthless. Our National Marine Fisheries Service has allocated to our vessel — next to nothing. They'll force us out - one way or another. "Listen, Dave," I told my hubby one night after supper. "Maybe our permits are worthless, but not the decades that we enjoyed fishing. Those years are priceless." David has a different view; he thinks its government run amuck.

When a man with an inshore dragger could choose where he needed to go, could choose what days to go out, and could choose what specie to target to make the most of the business, when men knew that kind of freedom, there was incentive to work, there was prosperity for many. Dave said to me today, "It feels strange to look around and see how few boats are left fishing. How did we manage to hang on? How come we made it through the years of cuts and cutbacks?"

I replied, "You're just too stubborn to give up fishing."

Dave and I know that it takes more than determination and faith to keep a fishing business profitable. Almost all of the rugged, self-sufficient, carefree, hardworking fishermen are gone from our town wharf; there was no parade, no confetti, no rewards, and no retirement benefits.

CHAPTER 12

Take Me Fishing

I'm a 'fair-weather' fisherman. It is Dave that keeps the *'Richard & Arnold'* running, maintained and afloat. He's got the fishermen's gene. I'm like so many others who love the oceans and are drawn to the sea, but spend little of my time actually working upon it. Once in a while I'll get lucky and Dave will say yes. Then I'll take a day or weekend out on the water, joining him for a fishing trip. He is always concerned that I will be uncomfortable, or get seasick. We leave our home in the pre-dawn hours and drive seven miles to the town wharf, climb down a sixteen-foot ladder, step gingerly onto the railing of the boat, and then jump a couple feet to the deck. I think about my moves. There is always a line made fast to a cleat from a boom or a wire to grab onto. David has drilled into me, "One hand for you and one hand for the ship."

As Dave takes the boat out of the harbor, I go below and make tea while checking out my cumbersome oil gear, rubber boots, and gloves made of neoprene to be sure all is dry. Then I will hang out in the wheelhouse to watch the water and sky.

Later before we set the net, I'll take Dave a couple of fried eggs with sausages, bread and more hot tea. When we reach that secrete place where Dave is hoping to find fish, he will take the boat out of gear and let me know that the work begins, "Time to set out."

After checking his view around the boat and in the radar screen, Dave will begin to heave the end of the net off the stern. I help where I can. The boat moves forward as the net is pulled from the spool, heavy from the iron doors, sinking out of sight. The speed of the boat is slow enough for a person to walk next to it if we were on land. I spend time on deck or in the wheelhouse going below to make lunch or snacks. Then after a set time — anywhere from 15 minutes to 2 hours the captain will holler, "Haul back. Now the fun begins." He gives me a smile of expectation. I love being there. I like picking the fish form the deck, but I'm not much help when it comes to the net and gear. "Let the machines do the lifting," Dave sings out to me.

The net is wound up on the drum of the spool and the fish are dumped from the bag onto the stern deck. Water drips from the net as I bend to the picking, lifting, measuring, sorting, washing, boxing and icing. One box at a time filling with fish, one hundred pounds to each box, I drag, never lifting, the boxes, across the wet deck. The fish are beautiful. With cold, clear, white foamy water running over the decks and out the scuppers, I work till my body is tired and then I rest. I know tonight I will sleep soundly, hoping my back won't ache in the morning. "We'll make this a 1 hour tow, let's get to sorting," Dave lets me know where to put the different sizes and different varieties. The noise of the engine is a constant and a welcome sound, like being on a bus for a while and I feel like there is just the two of us, alone in the world.

Sounds romantic and sometimes it is, like when it is calm and everything is going along without a hitch or breakdown, but most of the time fishing is just hard work. I try to keep my gloves dry because when your hands get wet they eventually swell, chafe and peel. My feet are heavy with boots as I squat, lean, bend, and shift my weight while I pick out the catch. Using a box hook, Dave will pull the totes across the deck to a grey plastic tub where we put the fish into iced salt water to be kept until unloaded at the wharf.

Dave loves his job and I like being out on the water, but I could never keep up with the rigorous work - for one day fishing is a joy, but two or more and I'll need a week to recover.

Last spring, Dave invited me to spend a weekend in Nantucket, not on shore in a guest house as would be nice, but onboard. It was his last weekend for squid and so I figured if I wanted to see the island this year I would have to fish for my holiday. He picked me up in Woods Hole and off we went, rocking and rolling our way up Nantucket Sound. A few boats were visible: ferries, fishing and sail, but it was not the summer days where many boats are moving across the water. The air was damp, pushing rain clouds our way and it was chilly. I was excited to be aboard, but as usual the motion of the waves made my stomach queasy. "We'll be fishing in the lee, and you'll feel better soon." I knew Dave was right so I just sat looking out at a gray sky waiting for calmer water. If fishing has taught me anything, it is patience. After an hour, we put the net out and began towing in the lee of Nantucket Island. "What are those specks of white across the water on the other side?" I asked pointing to the mainland. The dots looked almost indistinguishable from the land.

He picked up his binoculars and said, "Looks like a bunch of small sails near Hyannis."

We began our job of taking care of the squid that were slowly filling the boxes, the run of squid was just about over, and it had been a sparse year. I made a mid-morning snack and took it with tea to Dave. "Those specks look bigger." I said as I handed him the food. "Sailboats for sure," I said. Dave had moved the boat closer to the harbor entrance, in the lee of the island so that I wouldn't feel the wave action. For that my stomach and I were grateful. I watched the grey water, grey sky and the white sails on the horizon while I dug through a pile of sand looking for squid.

By two o'clock sail boats were coming into close visual range. The wind had picked up and Dave was getting ready to head into Nantucket Harbor. The last tow would end near the entrance of the harbor and his timing was just about perfect. The first of the sailboats were coming down into the narrow entrance of Nantucket Harbor - under full sail, leaning on their sides, straining from the strong winds, each boat racing toward an unseen finish line. Sailboats rushed past us, seeming to surround us. We were watching the 39th annual Figawi Race, from Hyannis to Nantucket and we had front row seats.

I had no idea that this event was happening when I'd signed on for a Memorial Day weekend of fishing, but Dave did and he was giving me a real treat. The '*Richard & Arnold*' remained in place as dozens of racing sailboats came soaring toward us. "They're not going to run into us in their desire to win are they?" I hollered out to Dave. Boats were now crossing our bow and stern within yards.

I was almost screaming with excitement. "I feel like a target."

Dave confidently said, "They are professional sailors, they should expect the unexpected. They can turn off if they have to." The racers flew by, boats of white, blue, green with colorful pennants flying in the mast tops, people sitting on the outside rail holding onto stay wires, clothed in the latest colorful foul weather gear, their faces white, eyes straining to see past the jetties into Nantucket Harbor, jetties that had width enough for only two boats passing at one time, while fifty knots of wind pushed and pulled them to the winners circle.

Later we walked around the piers where the racers were tied. "I'd love to do that," I told Dave. "Maybe someday we could trade in the fishing boat and get a sailboat." I made us fish cakes for supper that night and we talked about the sailor's life.

"If we give up fishing and go sailing you'll not be making fish cakes, you'll have to buy them," Dave said.

"There is that. I'd just be trading one adventure for another and I'd probably still get seasick, so I guess I'd rather be fishing." I told my captain.

My fish cakes haven't changed over the years, but our fishery sure has. When I cook I usually use a variety of ingredients. I like mixing it up, adding new foods and spices. Having a rich diversity in our food, our fisheries and in our way of life brings benefits to everyone. Without variety our world would be colorless, boring and without flavor, like never seeing a sailboat race. To have a fishery with only one type of boat, one method of catching and one point of view would mean the end of tradition, the end of free enterprise and the end of independence. I do not believe that a consolidated fishery with only a few large boats is a 'best use' policy for our fishery, but it is the way our government is heading.

I have a newspaper article from 'The New York Times', Sunday March 29, 1992. The headline reads, 'Can Snelling Brainard Sell His Global Fishing Vision?' The article describes an ideal corporate business. The American fisherman is obviously passé in this vision. The investors would buy boats, hopefully built in America and send them around the world to establish fishing fleets in developing nations. These boats would use long lines in places where there is little regulation - thousands upon thousands of feet of line with hooks or monofilament stationary gill nets, to catch fish. Each fleet would consist of thirty-two vessels. The smaller boats would bring the catch to the mother ship where the catch would be processed and delivered to global transportation depots. The fish could then be sold to Americans. This plan called for sharing forty-nine percent of company profits with the employees after 10 years. I wonder if those fishermen in Papua,

New Guinea are getting their share. I wonder if Mr. Snelling Brainard is still fishing. In this scenario, corporate American does not need the small fleets of this country. Greenpeace Organization stated that as of 2009 there is enough monofilament line in the water, to circle the globe 550 times. Maybe Mr.Brainard did realize his dream after all.

Every part of the fish is usable and every part of the catch is saleable. Fish are eaten; they are used to make certain vitamins, cosmetics, cat food and fertilizer - as well as for research. There is always a market looking for fish and shellfish, but many counties now grow fish in pens and export them to us, it's cheaper. Very little American seafood is sold abroad at this time - the National Marine Fisheries Service has restricted the catch to such low amounts that only a few boats in the Northeast Fishery are able to work. Some people believe that this is being done to force people to sell their permits - wealthier companies will be able to buy up the catch shares at low rates. Then, when the government opens fishing, having met the 'sustainable yields' — then the companies with all the catch shares will float to the top like foam. I wonder if it is just another coincidence that Mr. Locke, Director of National Marine Fisheries Service was appointed Ambassador to China, hopefully he won't sell our catch shares.

When it comes to fish there is a huge U.S. deficit, and I don't believe our government wants to see the American fisheries done away with, but it doesn't take a rocket scientist or an economic adviser to see that we are curtailing ourselves right out of business. If we could all just agree to agree that controls are necessary and fishermen should be allowed to fish, but that would be in a perfect world.

At a symposium at the Boston Aquarium dragger-men were labeled *"The most destructive force on earth"*. A prestigious presenter picked up a rubber roller (this is sometimes attached to the bottom of bigger nets) and dropped it on the floor of the stage. Because it weighs fifty pounds, it made a thunderous noise as it hit the stage and the audience jumped from there soft seats. He told the audience that this was what draggers were using to dig up the sea floor. He didn't explain about buoyancy and how this same roller barely touches the bottom; when fished correctly it bounces and floats and jumps over the bottom. It doesn't dig up the bottom like a dredge or rake. More importantly our '*Richard & Arnold*' has never used these rollers. This type of rolling gear is used in deep water to help keep the net near the bottom without hanging up on rocks or mountains of debris. Unfortunately some in the audience began to believe that fishermen might really be the most destructive force on earth, creating another reason to get rid of more fishermen and their boats.

There were many reasons for the down turn in the numbers of fish caught. Larger more efficient machine were created to catch and keep more and more of the fish stock, but also the loss of estuaries, the dumping of garbage into the water, a larger population living along the coast, these and more could have had significant impact. This speaker at the Boston Aquarium felt that the 'dragger' was at fault for all the woes of the oceans. Draggers were something that people could do something about: cut back on what they are allowed to catch, cut back on the number of fishing permits, cut back on the amount of time spent fishing, cut back on the number of men and the number of boats. It's working, there are very few boats and men working and the fish are back.

Over the years I have heard half-truths and misinformation used against the fishermen. I have witnessed one fishery pit against another and I have seen how radical environmentalists can spread the word that fishermen are destroying our seas. I watched as more than ninety percent (that's 90%) of the American fishing fleet disappeared. It is not a simple matter. In fact it is so complex that economists, scientists, environmentalists, lawyers, politicians and fishermen are trying to figure it out. The trouble is that each group seems to speak their own language, have their own agenda and their own set of rules. Perhaps as we learn more about each other and about our mysterious oceans, we will come to a new understanding about the fisheries as well. One can only hope.

I still haven't met the guy who has counted all the fish there are in the oceans, but I'd really like to. I have been told that the biomass is so low - that we will just have to eat the fish imported from Canada, Chile, Norway, New Guinea, and a dozen Asian and South American countries. Some people think we can buy it cheaper from them, but it actually is costing us in ways we are just beginning to understand. Our coastal communities are suffering. The small fleets brought more than fish to town, they brought jobs and money. The question is: how do we save the populations of fish and supply the people with high quality protein, while keeping our communities economically viable. The answer has always been: small boat, small capacity, owner/operated draggers — they are healthier for the fish, the environment and our coastal economy.

OK, if truth be told, there defiantly is need to control fishermen. Man has a way of getting better and better at what he does. Keep everyone happy and save planet earth, these are the struggles of politicos and bureaucrats. Fishermen just want to go fishing. In order to maintain a sustainable fishery, fishermen have to be controlled. Dave and I have always agreed with that. There are ways to balance our fishing heritage and the goal of sustainable fisheries, the United States is currently the only country in the world that is even close to approaching a sustainable fishery.

Our Provincetown fleet could manage when the ruling of 88 fishing days came along; that meant that everyone with a federal fishing license could fish this amount of time — in days. It seemed fair because everyone received the same allocation of time, the big boats with bigger nets caught more fish, but everyone had a chance. Then a buyback program was set up in which the government paid big money to buy fishing licenses to remove more boats and fishermen. This was a good way of ridding the industry of 'potential' effort and some dead beat permits. Our town saw a drop in the number of boats bringing fish to the wharf as men retired or sought work in other areas. Remember, every time a regulation, amendment or judgment is brought to us by National Marine Fisheries

Service, it affects the small-boat owner the same way it does the 120 foot offshore factory freezer ship.

Then along came the people from 'Oceans', 'Conservation Law Foundation', 'Audubon', 'Sierra Club', 'PETA', the 'Environmental Defense Fund', 'World Wildlife Federation' 'Pew Family Trust' and others who are, or have, or would like to sue National Marine Fisheries Service for what they are, or are not doing. Each group seems to be trying to rid our waters of fishing boats. They have lawyers and lobbyists who keep up the rhetoric about how bad those draggers are. Small-boat fishing families don't stand a chance. The bureaucracy has grown exponentially, while our fishing businesses have shrunk. I am not saying that these organizations do not have high ideals, but when any group assumes its own superiority over others - they usually begin by removing what doesn't correspond to their beliefs in how the world should look. Or as John Locke (1632-1704) said, "Men see a little, presume a great deal, and so jump to conclusions."

In the kid-friendly movie "<u>Finding Nemo</u>," there is a character that recites "Fish are our friends, not food." Is this some kind of joke; our friends? If they were my friends then I'd have to try and stop them from eating each other. Most of the NGO's and active environmental groups ask that you send money to protect our oceans. I agree we need to protect ourselves from greed, avarice, and gluttony, but believe it or not, Dave and I don't think you need protection from us, and you don't have to send money.

The Department of Commerce, NOAA, National Marine Fisheries Service, the agency that rules our lives, began to dissect every aspect of the fishery in the early 1970's. Jargon and legalese has become part of our working dialect. There are acronyms for every agency and bureau on both State and Federal levels. There are offices burgeoning with paper work. Each agency comes with its own initials. How about: the EEZ-LMA for NMFS –DAS branch of NOAA which has authority over NE Multispecies Permit Office of the DOC. Or the NEFMRWRT, which I think stands for the North East Fishery Management Right Whale Recovery Team. The point is that many new groups - both government and non-government - were formed on the backs of the commercial fishermen. The acronyms have established a whole new language, just dealing with fish. While creating the agencies to deal with the ever growing knowledge of what men are capable of, the little guys got caught up, dare I say, "Like fish in a net." Our business is smaller today than when we started because we have been forced, over and over and over to give up: fishing time, areas, catch amounts, catch species- for the betterment of the future of the fishery. Twenty years ago I told Dave that we should not give up fishing, I told him things would get better, we would be rewarded for our efforts of conservation. I didn't believe anyone had the right to take away our fishing heritage. Now I scratch my head and wonder if we've made the right choice.

"WOW!" I told Dave. "If that guy at the Boston Aquarium is right, you have the power! Just think. To be the Number 1 force on earth. What domination! Imagine moving tides with your mind, shifting sands with a wave of a finger, filling up the net with a pass of the hand." I gave my husband a big hug, a big kiss and a pat on the back. "You must be one of God's gifts, well, at least to me you are." That man at the aquarium and others like him, have helped squeeze us into a very tight corner. If we really are all that omnipotent, then we must be one of the most valuable commodities on Earth as well - the American Fishermen.

My Recipe for Fish Cakes: **Wash a codfish or haddock, remove fins and steam in a couple of inches of salted water for 10 minutes. Cool, remove skin & bones. Place the fish in a large bowl — add one chopped onion, one egg, and an amount of shredded potatoes equal to the fish. Add 1 tsp. of Cumin, then salt and pepper to taste. Mix. Make patties the size of the palm of your hand. Dust fish cakes with flour, dip in beaten egg, and then dip into bread crumbs, I use Panko. Fry in hot oil. Enjoy!**

CHAPTER 13

Fishing for a Future

There are still a few commercial boats tied to McMillan Wharf, some have lobster licenses, some have only state permits and there are six boats with Federal Fishing Permits. Of those six, only <u>one</u> currently has enough cod-fish allocation to make it profitable and that boat is a gill-netter from Chatham. The five Provincetown boat owners who have retained their federal permits should congratulate each other for being able to continue in this business, if you call this continuing - because the effort that has been used to get rid of us - has kept groups, agencies and government offices employing thousands and thousands of people for over thirty years.

Our historic dragger has been tied to the wharf for six months while people from the Environmental Defense Fund and Sea Change Investment Fund divide up the fish stocks into shares. At the rate we are going the American northeast fishery will end up with a couple of very large boats owned by very large corporations. Americans pushed out the Russian factory trawlers with the passing of the Magnuson/Stevens

Act in 1976, which set the 200 Mile limit. The Magnuson Stevens Act specifically states that the 'sustained participation of such (fishing) communities be provided for' and that 'adverse economic impacts on such communities be minimized'. The Russians left. We were told it was because they were too big and would deplete the stock. Now we are told that corporate fishing is more efficient. The adverse economic impact on our fishing community in Provincetown has reach epic proportion, our fishing families have left, our high school is closing, our fishing fleet is diminished and our heritage is all but gone.

When the Feds allocated the monkfish or goosefish as we've always called them, they mailed us an application which we promptly filled out and which was promptly returned requesting we provide proof that our vessel had caught monkfish. For our first ten years of fishing and scalloping we used to throw monkfish back, kick them out the scuppers, because there was no market for them. They lived, by the way, because they were only on deck for a few minutes before being pushed out the scupper with all the other stuff nobody would eat. It was trash fish. There was no market for many types of fish at that time, Americans didn't eat goosefish tails. We began keeping and selling monkfish when an overseas market was created in the 1980's. Where was our paperwork to prove that we had caught monkfish? It was buried in boxes in the garage. At the time this license was lost to us, we were living with David's mom who had Alzheimer's disease and his father who was dying from Parkinson's disease. Our home was being reno-

vated to allow mom to live with us, so we had all our belong-
ings stored in the garage. There, under our collection of 10
years of household stuff were the boxes that showed we landed
goosefish. Could we have proved that we had landed monkfish? You bet. Did we? No. Our apathy was at an all-time low.

Our records predate computer generated printouts,
but the government's steamrollers of time keep pressing forward. It is as if our fishing fleets are living in a time warp, in
a period for which there is no history and we Americans allow
non – government – organizations (NGO's) to take over the
fishing industry in a subtle way, using terms that most people
would agree with: environmental defense, efficiency, sustainability, increased profits. Unfortunately, their efforts are really self-serving.

National Marine Fisheries Service began getting sued by
these same NGO's in the 1980's - for just about everything:
the oceans were depleted, the U.S. was moving too slow, the
world needed to be monitored more closely, fish populations
needed studying and counting, whales needed protecting, the
sky was falling. It became a mantra and a mandate; the taking
of fish would be regulated to the strictest measure to ensure
a sustainable future. The NGO's didn't tell you it would be
them making money on the fish stocks once they were rebuilt.

A man named Max sued the State of Massachusetts; stat-
ing he "spoke for the whales." He won his case and millions
of dollars are now spent yearly protecting these mammals. I'm
100 % in favor of leaving these beautiful sea creatures alone,
but what is not told, what is misrepresented is that small

draggers like ours never catch whales. Never! I can't speak for other types of fishing, like gill nets and long-lines, but our dragger has never molested a whale, we move slowly, and we take our gear home with us. I have read articles where a whale was found entangled in 'fishing gear'- everyone jumps to the conclusion that draggers are the culprit. We are not!

One day while fishing on the far side of Cape Cod Bay, Dave called out to me, "See what that is off the starboard bow up ahead, looks like something floating on the water." It was summer and we were moving through the water at four knots. I had been lying on the fish hatch sunning myself. Dave took the boat out of gear and we drifted in the direction of a mass of what looked like a camouflaged boat just under the surface. I was out on the bow hanging on a stay wire looking down at what I thought was a submarine.

"WOW!" I hollered to Dave, "hurry up and take a look at this. WOW", I kept yelling, "WOW, WOW Holy Mackerel!" He was standing next to me in seconds; we were suspended above the giants, next to the side of the boat, a few yards from me were three Whale Sharks.

Their backs were about thirty feet long and at first we didn't know what they were doing. These creatures were slow, languid and completely unafraid of our small fishing boat, but I had the feeling that if they wanted they could cripple or even sink our vessel. Whale Sharks! These massive creatures feed on plankton like whales, but strain water out through gills, like fish. They are extremely rare in Cape Cod Bay and must have strayed in on tides from the Gulf Stream that summer.

We see Humpback and Right Whales all the time when out fishing, like going to work in your car and seeing a school bus; they are sometimes a part of the scenery. We don't bother them and they don't bother us. Watching them gives me a strange and awesome feeling; there is a uniqueness about them that supercedes my understanding. The ocean is so powerful, so full of mystery and life that I cannot help but be amazed and wondrous of it all.

Predatory behavior by other marine animals is rarely spoken of. Natural predaceous plunder by seals is rarely mentioned when talking of fish populations. It's a touchy subject because people think seals are so cute. Sure they have big eyes and you'd like to take them home as pets, but here is an eye opener: a census taken in 2001 put the seal population - sunning themselves on Monomoy Island off Chatham, Massachusetts - at about 3000 seals. Each adult seal eats 20 pounds of meat (fish) per day. That's 60,000 pounds a day for the seals on Monomoy in 2001.

In 2009, a seal count put the population on Monomoy Island at approximately 12,000. That is approximately 86,000,000 pounds of fish eaten by seals each year, in one small area on Cape Cod, and usually they are eating the smaller juvenile fish that have yet to spawn. We might starve to death, but the seals will be healthy and fat. I wonder how long it will take before we start eating seal meat. I hear it's pretty good. In 1960, seals were rare on Monomoy Island and a man was rewarded with a $5.00 bounty for each seal he killed. We never had a great white shark problem before either — now the sightings of these mammoth beasts are a daily occurrence, and tourists are told to stay out of the water. I am not advocating a seal hunt, just hoping for some perspective on the fishing industry.

There is a proposal to close the middle bank (Stellwagen Marine Sanctuary) to all fishing, a place of abundance, and an historic fishing ground. The reasons are unclear, but someone thinks it must be better for the planet. So now we are going to protect the underwater sand dunes from fishermen, give all the fish to the seals and import what we need to eat from places where it is being grown in fish pens from third world counties, while our scrubbed-clean Americans can only guess at what rules and regulations are used there.

We always figured the boat and business (the Federal fishing license that we held onto so dearly) would be worth some retirement money, like a taxi cab medallion in NYC. It should be worth something, shouldn't it? We received 32.4 days at sea when the NMFS took away the equality of (88) eighty eight days and replaced it with the amount of effort used. I think if we had known what was happening; Dave would have put in as much effort as he possible could, as some men did. But we got involved in growing sea scallops and taking care of aging, ill parents. Today when we aren't allowed to catch enough fish to make a loan payment, how could a young man make a living at it? Who would want to buy this business? Our medallion is worth very little.

But it gets worse.

With every passing year came new closures, both permanent and something called a 'rolling closures'. We can only go where there are open areas and most of the year that means we have to first travel hours or days to get to the fishing grounds that are open. When we had the "call in and out" system, the clock started before you left the dock. Now the clock starts when your vessel goes across a demarcation line. Here in the Northeast we are being charged two hours for every hour fished- that's if you go into the Gulf of Maine, our backyard. Remember, effort equals allocation and as we were curtailed so our allocation grew less.

I'd have to say that my all-time favorite program brought to us by our government is the 'Observer Program'. We were told that it would help fishermen and that it was for our own good. They said that understanding more about the catch would help understand how to rebuild a shrinking industry. Like many government backed programs, it was controversial, thought to be experimental, but as it turns out — it was costly and intrusive as well. I can understand the need to watch fishermen, I like watching them.

The government was right to keep their eyes on this industry. As Linda Greenlaw said, "All fishermen are liars" and Dave tells me, "You can tell when a fisherman is lying; his lips are moving." Our government negotiated with a private company to hire workers to go out with vessels while they fished. This company has as its CEO, a man who retired as director of Northeast Regional Office of the National Marine Fisheries Service, I'm sure that's just a coincidence. These observers write down statistics on each tow, measuring fish, noting discards, and marking other information that would produce a data base. I am sure that most of the observers have good intentions, needing a job or some adventure; some may even be young biologists in training or may even grow up to be Deputy Director of the Massachusetts Division of Marine Fisheries. Who knows!

The program has developed over the years into another powerful group that has authority over fisherman. Dave has had to swallow his pride and take them on board whenever they want to go out with him. They show up on the wharf at dawn carrying boots and backpack. One morning a man who looked like he had been living in his car and couldn't climb a ladder if his life depended on it, came up to Dave and said, "I'm with the Observer Program and I'm going fishing with you." No ifs ands or buts, about it. When Dave came home from that trip he said to me, "It's like letting a stranger into our home. The guy was green, puked over the side most of the day and didn't know one fish from another. I can't imagine what he wrote on his notepad for that day's catch?"

I sometimes feel sorry for these nice young men and women who are trying to supplement their income. Part of our problem with this program is that you have to notify the program managers in advance so they can send someone to be at the dock early in the morning. The Observers sometimes drive hundreds of miles from their homes to make the fishing trip. This year Dave will need to call their office forty-eight hours in advance of leaving to go fishing. The problem is that

Dave doesn't know if he's going out until he gets up in the morning and steps outside to see what the wind is doing "How can I tell them what I don't know?"

Fishermen often complain they are being treated like criminals and now a stranger (via the Observer Program) has the right to take away our livelihood. Last time Dave had an Observer come on a fishing trip the man came with a check list and after taking inventory he told Dave to tie up the boat because his flare kit was one month over the expiration date. Dave was not allowed to go fishing until his flare kit was replaced. The closest place to buy one would be Chatham's Fishermen Supply. It would take the rest of the morning to get the kit. When the Observer left, Dave was furious. Then he remembered that our son, Robert, whose boat was hauled out for the winter, would have a flare kit. The observer had already left, so Dave borrowed our son's flares and went fishing, but he worried all day that he'd be fined for not taking the observer. We have witnessed what can happen when you refuse an observer.

Our friend Bobby went berserk, like a madman because of an observer. One spring squid season the *'Four-Kids'* was tied to the dock in Woods Hole. Bobby, the owner and captain was sound asleep in his bunk when a man came aboard. Bobby woke to this stranger standing over him. He jumped up screaming, "Who the hell are you? Get the f—k off my boat." The stranger told him he was with the Observer Program and he was going fishing with him that day. Well Captain Bobby freaked out. His curses could be heard all over the wharf. He

let that fellow know in no uncertain terms that he was tres-
passing, he didn't give a good God damn who he was and that
he should get the hell off his boat before he threw him into
the water. The young man backed away and left the boat, but
Bobby continued yelling. Dave told me he'd never seen anyone so mad.

The observer's face drained to a pure white as he stood
on the wharf taking this verbal onslaught. Dave, hoping to de-
fuse the explosive hostility, volunteered to take the 'Observer'
out for the day. The observer stepped aboard the *'Richard &
Arnold'* and off they went fishing.

Later that morning, Bobby took his boat out fishing and
when he returned to the dock the environment police, the
coast guard and local police were waiting for him. His catch
was confiscated, he had to pay a fine and his operator's license was revoked for six months. If Dave had known that the
observer was going to make a big stink about the incident he
would never have taken him out. Dave said to me, "I'd have
stayed in and lost the day before I would have let that punk put
Bobby out of business." There's a lesson to be learned here:
don't piss off an observer; if he wants to go fishing, you take
him. I believe the Gestapo used the same tactics. You have no
rights and you can't say no.

The sea scallop Observer Program uses other (legal?)
means to get what they want, but I still don't know what it is
they want. They have rules that say if you pay to take an Observer on a scalloping trip, around $700 dollars per trip, you
can take three times the limited amount of scallops per trip.

Without an Observer on board, a boat can bring in four hundred pounds per day. With an Observer the boat gets to keep twelve hundred pounds. Sounds like extortion to me. Too bad this doesn't work with fish. If the government would allow us to keep more fish we might just want those Observers on board, even if we had to pay them.

We are unsure of what will come next. I have wished for a crystal ball, because we never know what is going to happen next, what plans our government has for us. When Frank Parson brought the '*Richard & Arnold*' to Provincetown in 1927 fish supported a crew of five. Today it is almost impossible to support just the captain and it is not because we couldn't catch the fish to make it profitable, it is because we are not allowed — or the allocation is too small. The '*Richard & Arnold*' is being forced out of the fishing business after all.

This once honorable profession has been dragged down, beaten, derided, choked, spat upon, lied about, lied to, and is finally in the throes of death. The fisherman of today is on display as an environmental terrorist. He is feared or ignored, envied and romanticized about. If there is something amiss in the ocean, blame the fishermen, don't mention increased populations building on every inch of coastline, don't talk about pollution, road run off into estuaries, dumping garbage in the canyons off New York and New Jersey, don't bring up the fact that 85 % of our estuaries have been closed to spawning fish by tract homes and condo development, just point the finger at the fall guy and then this society that is so good at crisis intervention can put the minds of its people to rest and its finger in the dyke.

You'll always be able to buy fish. With tighter control the price will rise and the biggest players will reap the benefits. I am pleased to see that many fish stocks are rebuilding now that effort has been so drastically reduced. In many ways, intervention began in 1985 with the statement, "We're from the Federal Government and we're here to help you." Since that day I have been waiting for that help. Since that time we have been getting mailings weekly, with new proposals for more effort reductions. Since that time the effort reduction has gone beyond the 50% that was called for, it is more like 98 % and there is no end in sight. We have had to fight for the right to keep fishing.

Knowing what modern factory boats can do, Dave and I agree that there is a need to control the taking of fish. Just look at the size of the vessels in the TV hit show, 'Deadliest Catch'. You could put the Richard & Arnold' on the deck of the 'Wizzard' and they could keep fishing. In some cases, bigger is better. I'd not go fishing in the Bearing Sea in anything less.

There is a book entitled, <u>Commercial Fishing</u> by Herbert Zim and Lucretia Krantz, published by William Morrow & Co in 1973. The first page states that "there are over a million and a half boats at sea searching for fish and that some of these ships are 700 feet long." WOW! I've never seen anything like that, but if there are fishing boats 700 feet long then no wonder there's nothing left. We chose to fish with the traditional small fishing boat instead of getting bigger like many of our neighbors. We could have, but I like having my husband home at night as much as possible. Dave and I like our old boat, it's comfortable and we've always been able to catch enough to keep our heads above water, making an honest decent living. Like everything in the fishing world and the great oceans, things are about to change again.

Dave and I agree that it might be time to leave fishing. How can we fight, pit ourselves against the Environmental Defense Fund and PEW Foundation? We are both fighting mad about what has happened to the business we love, but the end of the line is near. A mailing from our National Marine Fisheries Service came the other day; we have been given an allowance of 640 pounds of sea scallops for the entire year. That's our total allowable catch for the whole year. I feel so insulted.

Dave and I are the only people in Massachusetts who have caught wild sea scallop seed known as spat, growing them out in bags and cages for an aquaculture research project in Cape Cod Bay. We had successes and failures growing sea scallops, learning from our experiences. After catching millions of spat and larvae by hanging bags in the water column we now know what can and cannot be done to grow Sea Scallops. Much of the project was successful, but predation by sea creatures as well as by our fellow man made it impossible to continue. As an experiment it was a success, but financially it didn't pay. The money expended didn't match the money coming in. I know how to catch, grow and cultivate sea scallops, I know what they eat, how they reproduce, when they move and how, I know where in the world they are being grown and how long it takes to grow the product. Today for all our hard work, experience and for all our history in the scallop industry- we have been allocated 640 pounds of sea scallops for the year.

Those years when we loaded the *'Wildflower'* with scallops, trip after trip- count for nothing. The years we spent sea scalloping with the *'Richard & Arnold'* count for nothing. How does our government justify allocating only 640 pounds a year of sea scallops to the *'Richard & Arnold'*? They used a time frame when our boat was busy in other areas like growing sea scallops. To be honest – I have to say that I am not just angry; I am disappointed in my country.

Our government has narrowed the field of northeast commercial fishing vessels from thousands to a few hundred with plans to cut back even more. 'Sector Management' was pushed as supporting our fishermen, to help fishermen control their own allocation, but it is so complicated that most fishermen don't really understand what it means to the future of fishing. It is a method of consolidation. Sector management is based on catch shares and catch shares are based on how much you caught during a determined period of time. The more you caught during the years 1996 through 2006, the more your share of the fish pie. This may sound like a logical way of distributing the fishing wealth, but for hundreds of fishermen the method used for determining how much fish you are allowed –is unfair and unjust. Catch shares will profit those with enough money, who will buy out fishermen like David and I - whose small allocations won't be enough to pay for the cost of a haul-out, much less support a family. Most of the smaller inshore boats have been given such tiny shares that they will not be able to make a profit from fishing and will be forced to sell out to those who can afford to buy. This is being done to drive the consolidation of the fishery. Dave explained to me how this is supposed to work. "If we had enough money and could find someone to sell us their share, we could buy our fish before we catch it." Somehow I can't wrap my mind around the concept of paying someone before I catch them. What if I don't catch them? Being a New Englander, a Cape Codder, an independent American fisherman, Dave can't believe he has to buy fish from someone sitting in an office, so that he can make money on fish that Dave has not yet caught. It seem unjustifiable, something that goes against the grain, like putting salt into the wound.

The NMFS calls it consolidation. I call it un-American. David and I have been put out of work by our own government. We are a part of the unforeseen consequences, the results brought to fishermen in the form of regulations aimed at a sustainable fishery. I compare the work ethics of the fishermen that I have known to that of the farmer: they both greet the day early, fix with their own hands what needs repair, harvest enough to keep the business going and pray for good weather. It isn't just the boats that have disappeared - it is the community, comradeship and spirit of industry.

"As it turns out there are more fish in the ocean than we previously believed," Professor Steve Murawski retired in 2010 as head scientist with NOAA / NMFS, now a professor at the University of South Florida has stated in an article released by the Associated Press on January 9, 2011, "Over fishing in New England will be a thing of the past by the end of 2012. This is not just a decadal milestone, but a century phenomenon." He then talks about the 'catch share system' that has cut the number of boats fishing in New England from 1200 to 580. He is one of many scientists who are speaking out in favor of giving relief to the commercial fishermen of New England in the form of more catch allotment.

We don't regret choosing fishing as a way of life, but I do regret having our way of life stolen from us by agencies that were meant to protect its citizens. The fishing industry is morphing into another American corporate giant and the winners will take it all. The oceans are an alien world of eat or be eaten and now man is gobbling up as much as he can of its bounty for bigger shares and bigger profits. Is the Richard & Arnold obsolete, inefficient, a dinosaur in our own time? Maybe, but still I ask myself, "Where have all the boats gone? Where have all the fishermen gone? What happened to an industry that fed millions and supported whole communities?" If we continue along this course we will become sharecroppers, begging for a share from the wealthy fish barons. It doesn't have to be this way.

As Americans we can create a mandate, an Act or addition to the Amendment or special legislation that will prevent the last of her kind from disappearing over the horizon. I propose an exemption - to include any permits that have been continually fishing for over 40 years. I propose that these permits have special privileges, should be allowed to fish the way they were intended, should be allowed to participate in the American dream. I propose that America include an historic category to the Sustainable Fisheries Act, or give us our rightful history. I am hopeful and positive that we can find a way to protect the few remaining traditional fishing businesses. Nautical twilight has come and gone - and yes, it is a changing world, but there is right and there is wrong and that should be enough.